This Book Belongs To...

~~Ella Alun~~
Ava

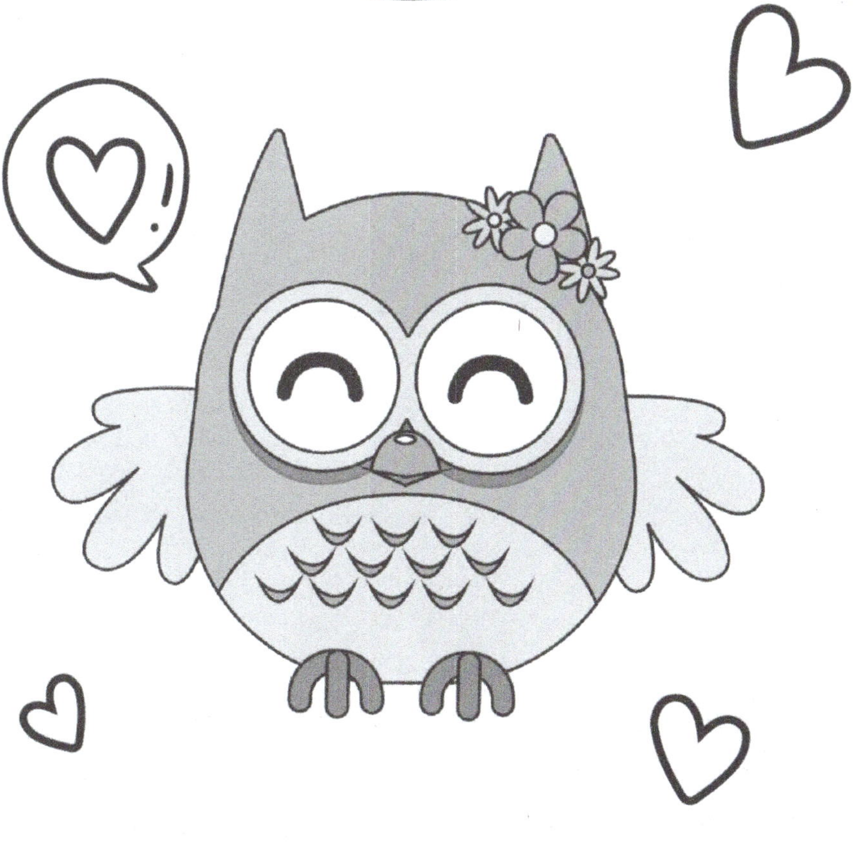

10/1/2022

Happy Birthday, Ella! I hope you have the best year & future years to come. Remember that you are fabulous ☺

♡ The Johnsons

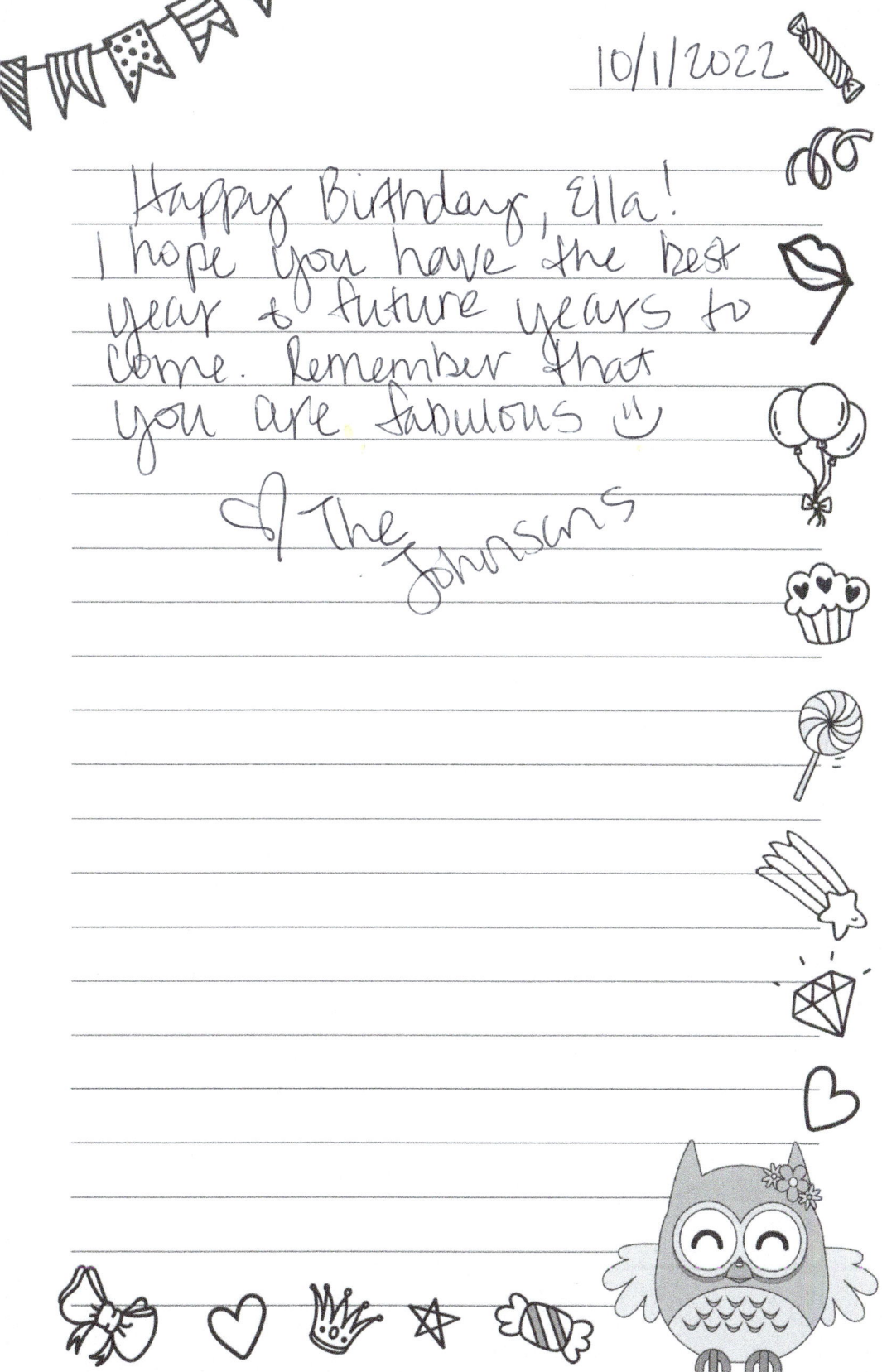

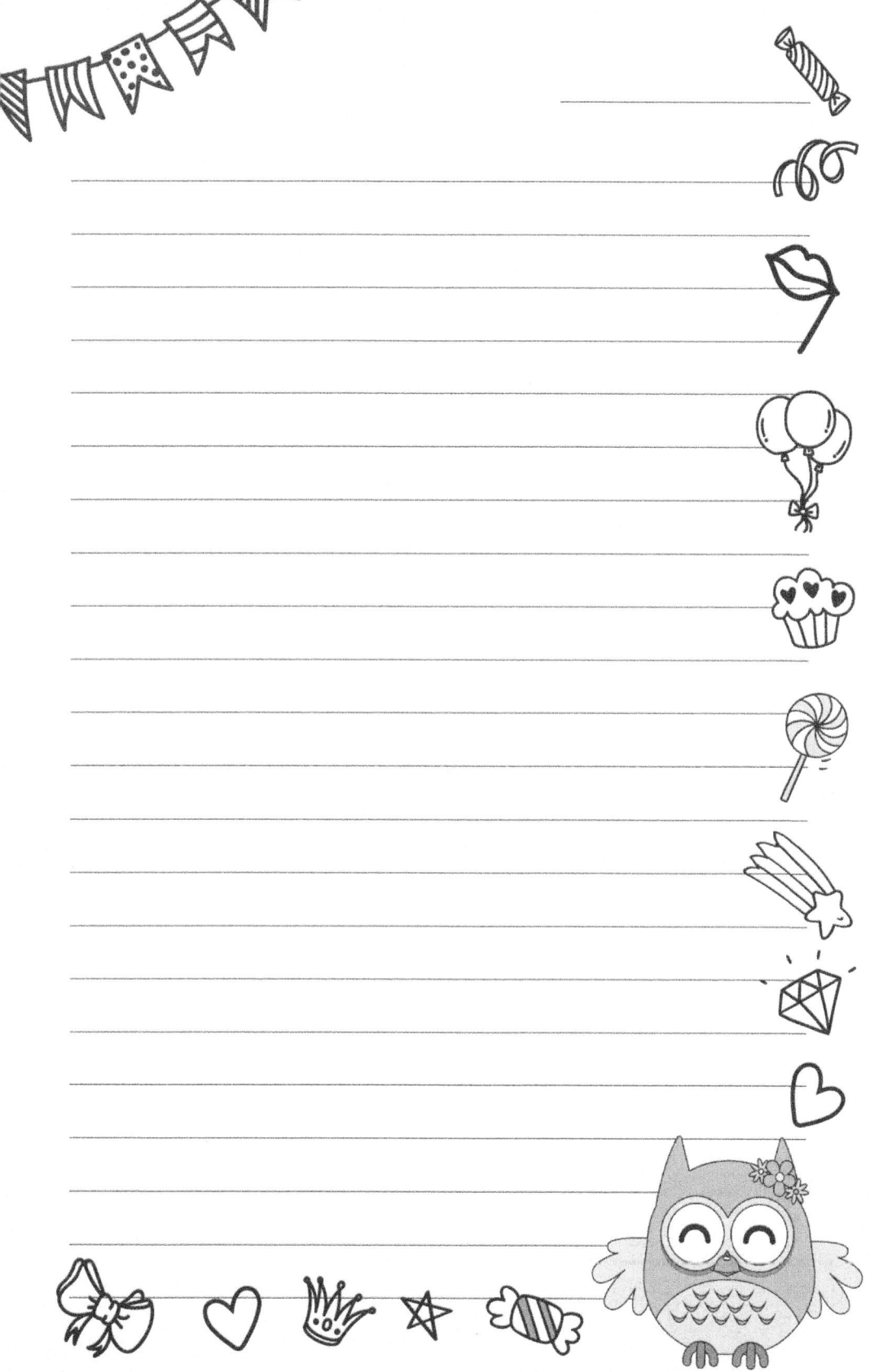

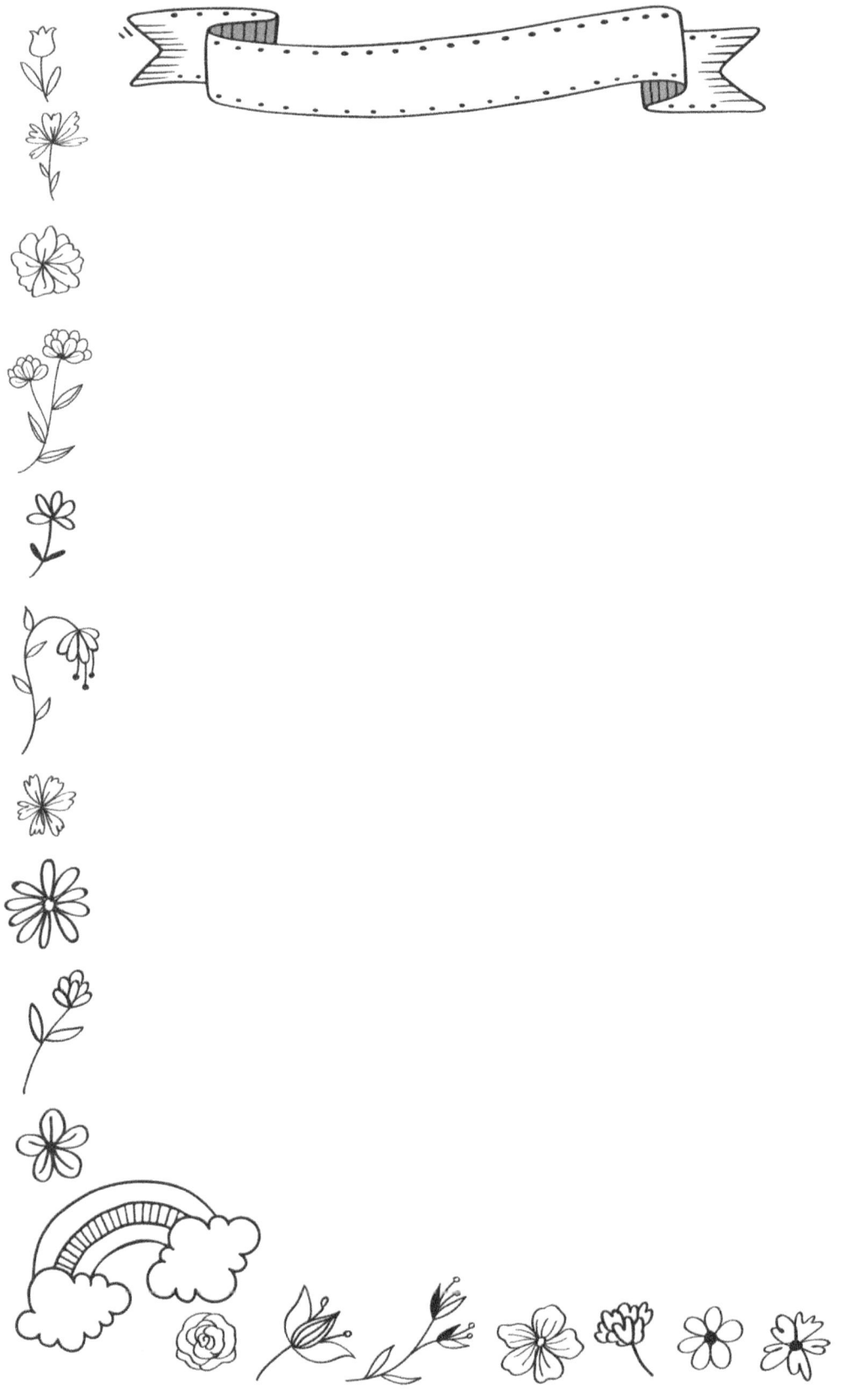

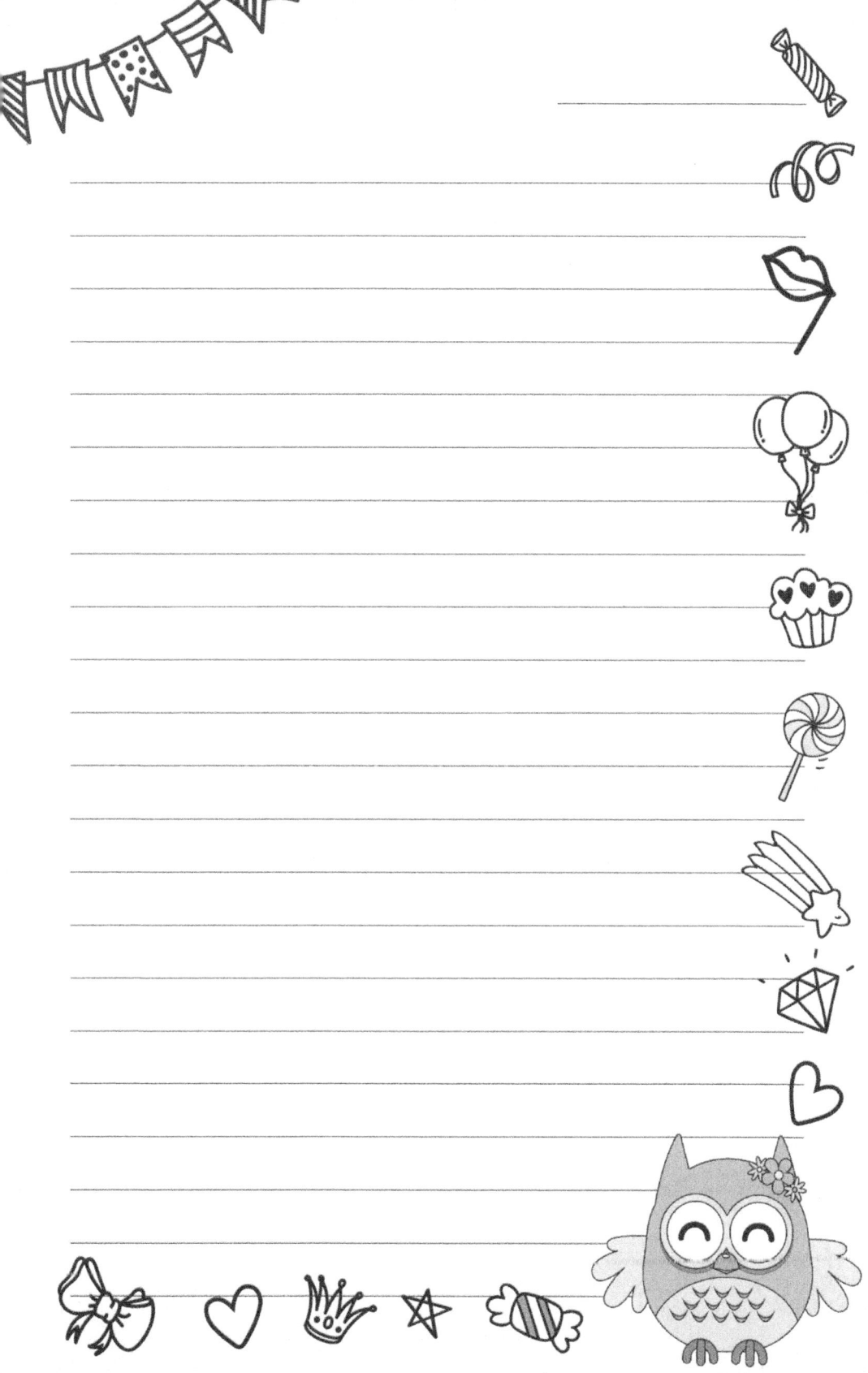

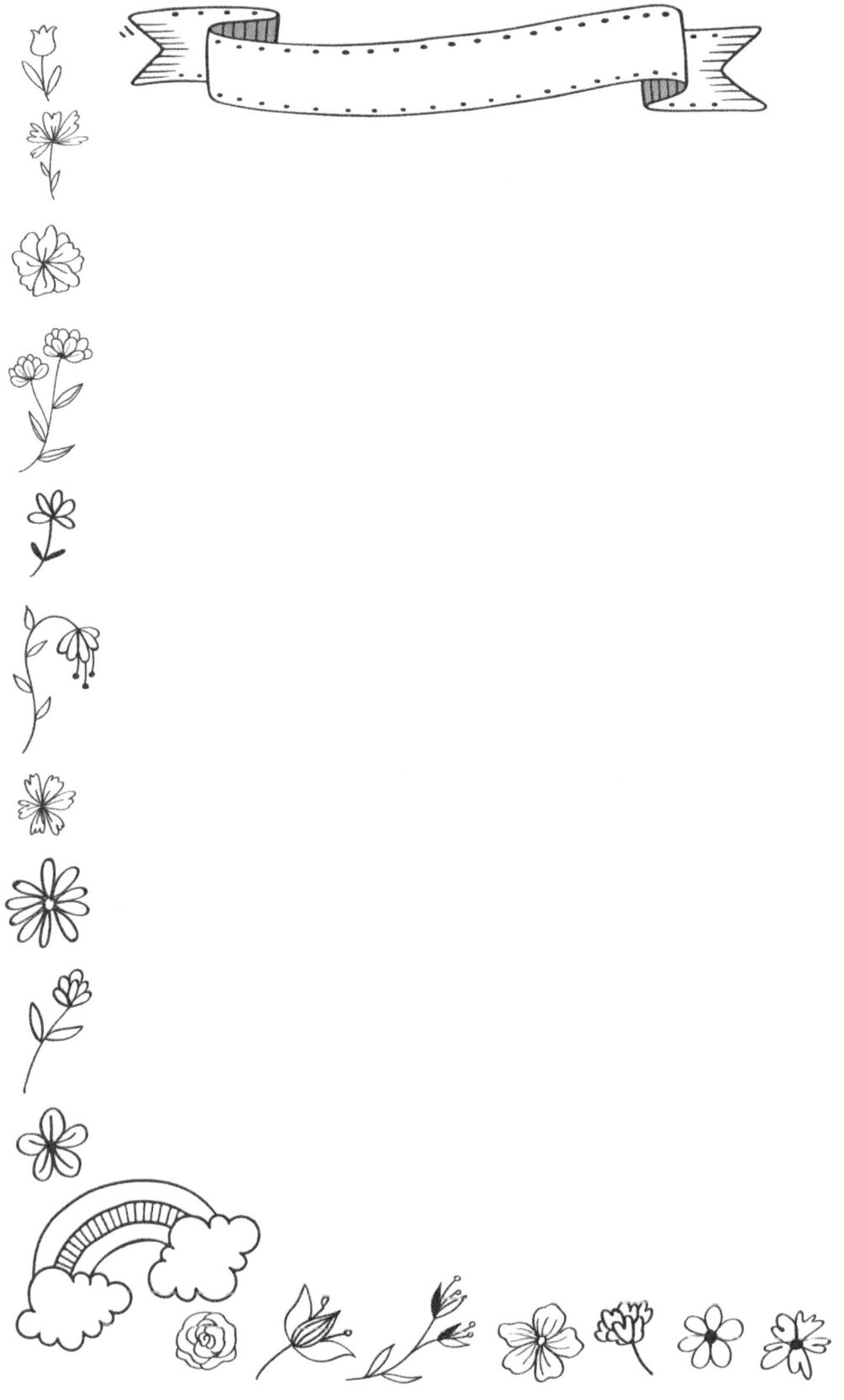

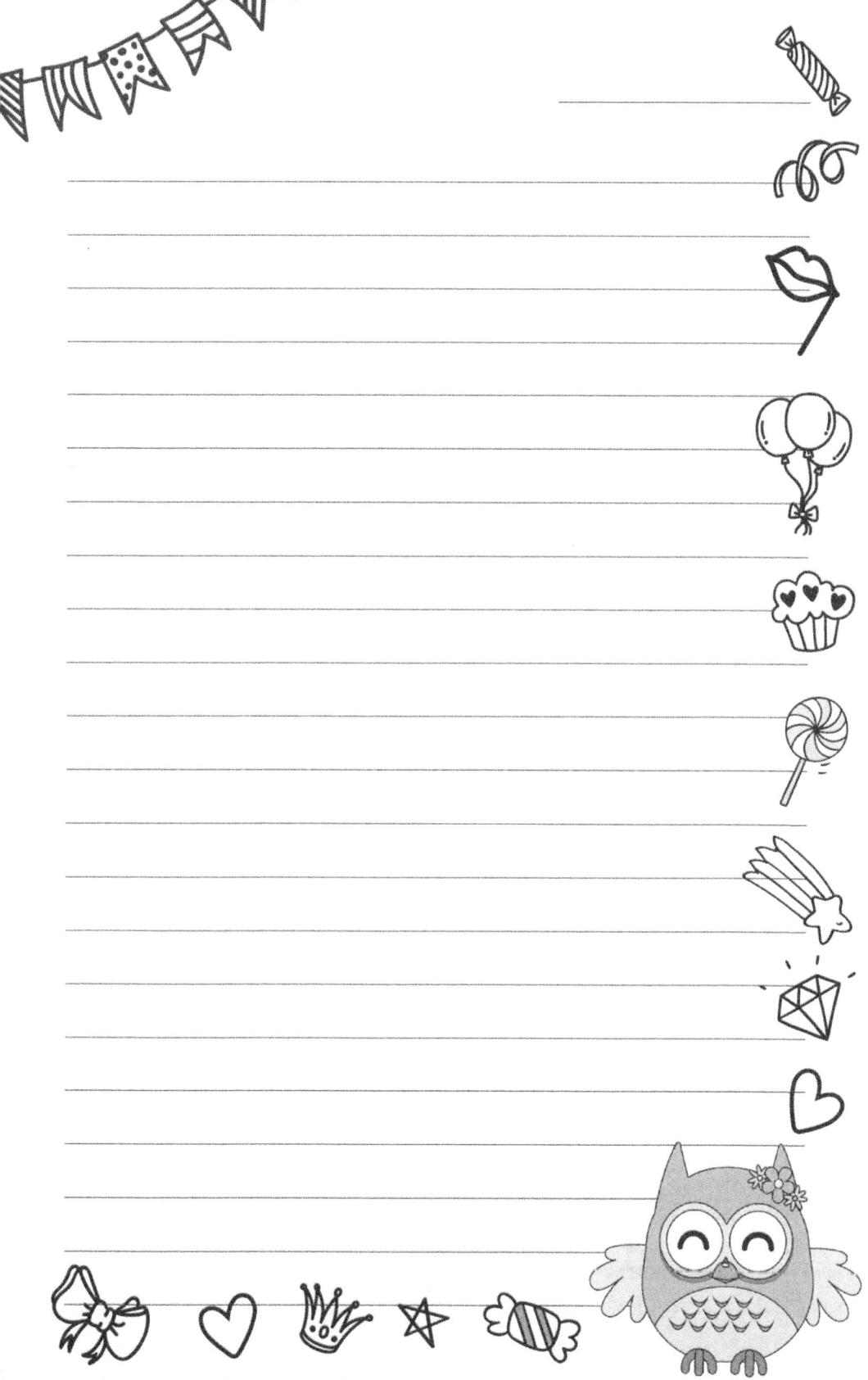

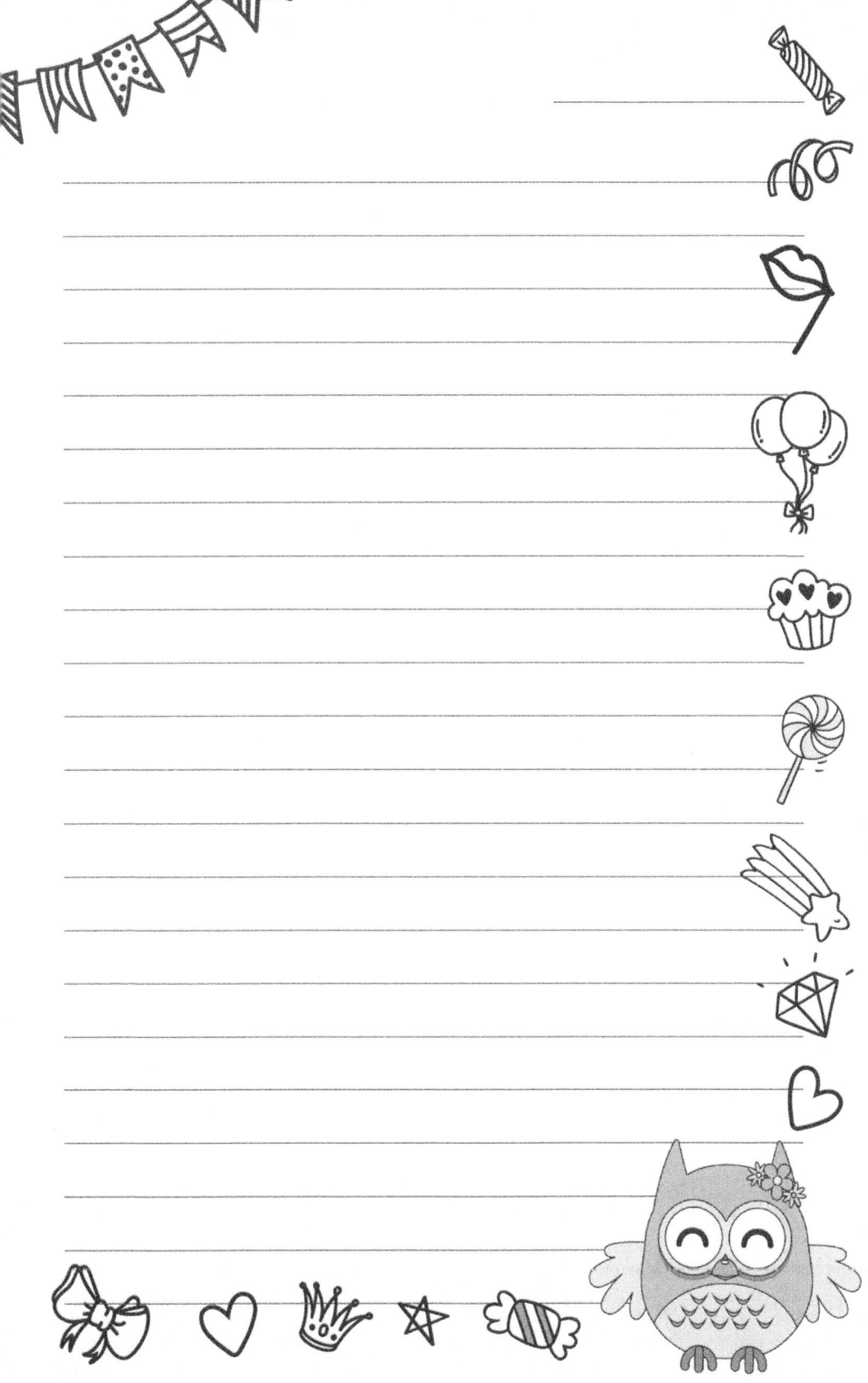

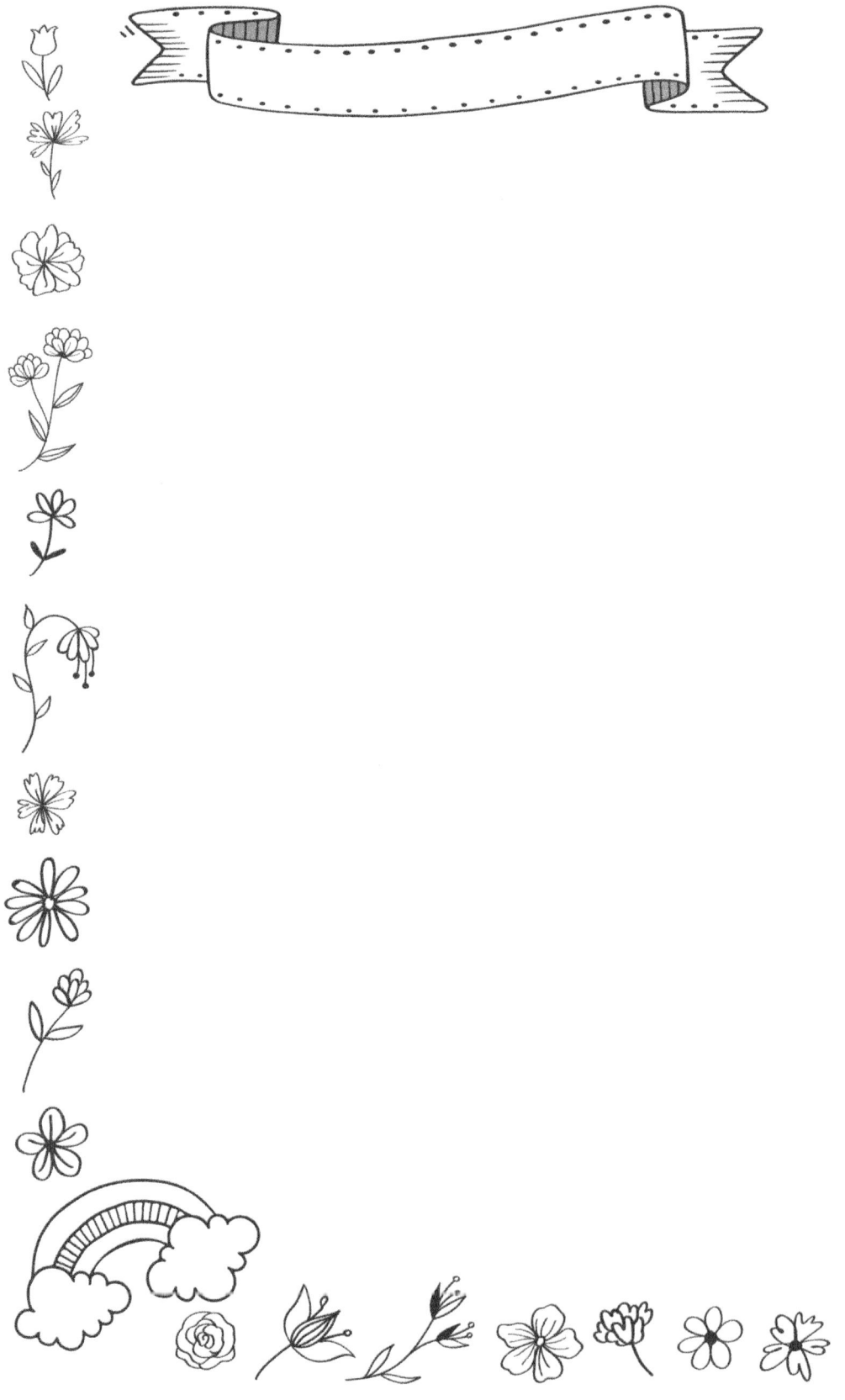

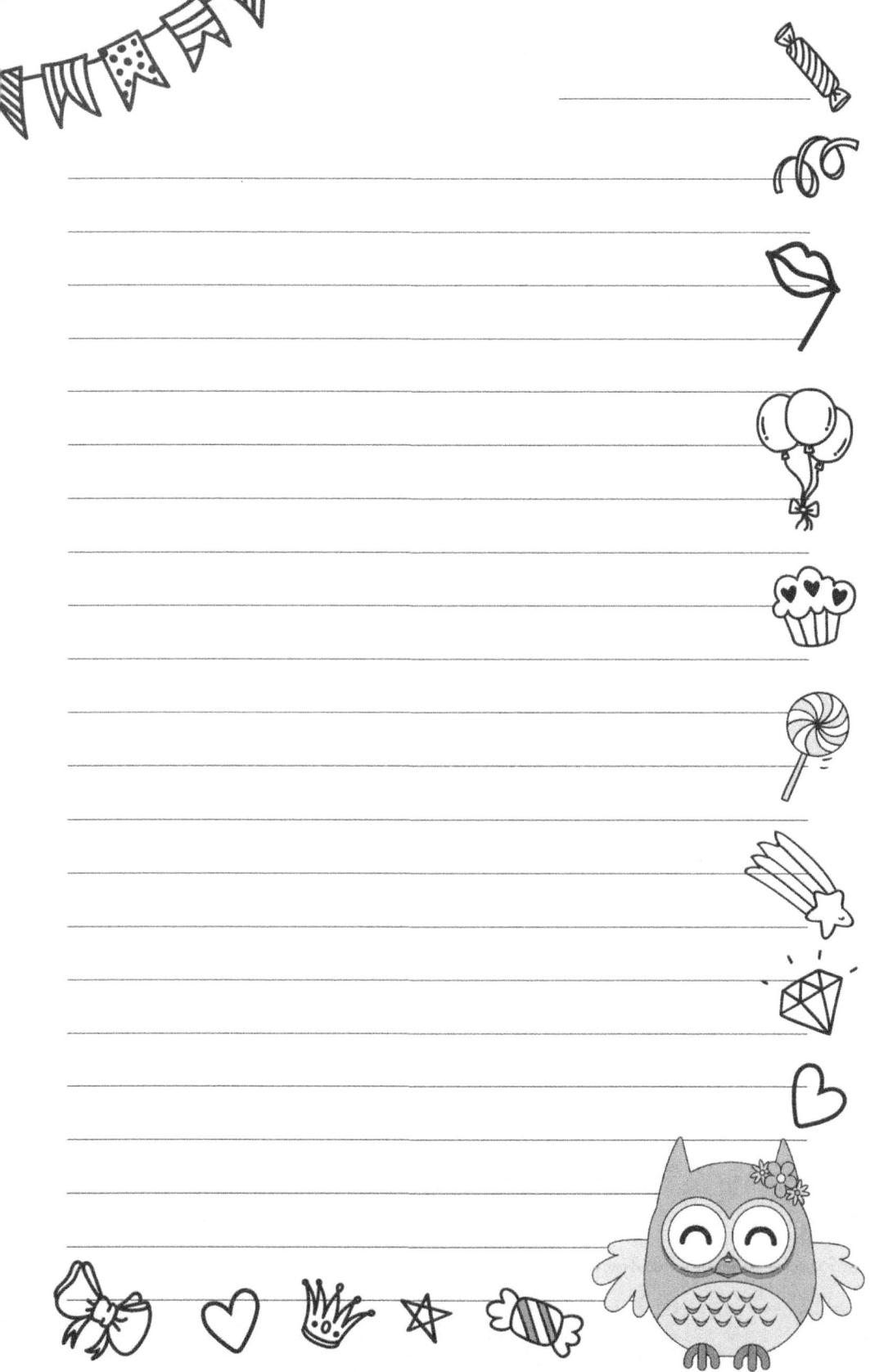

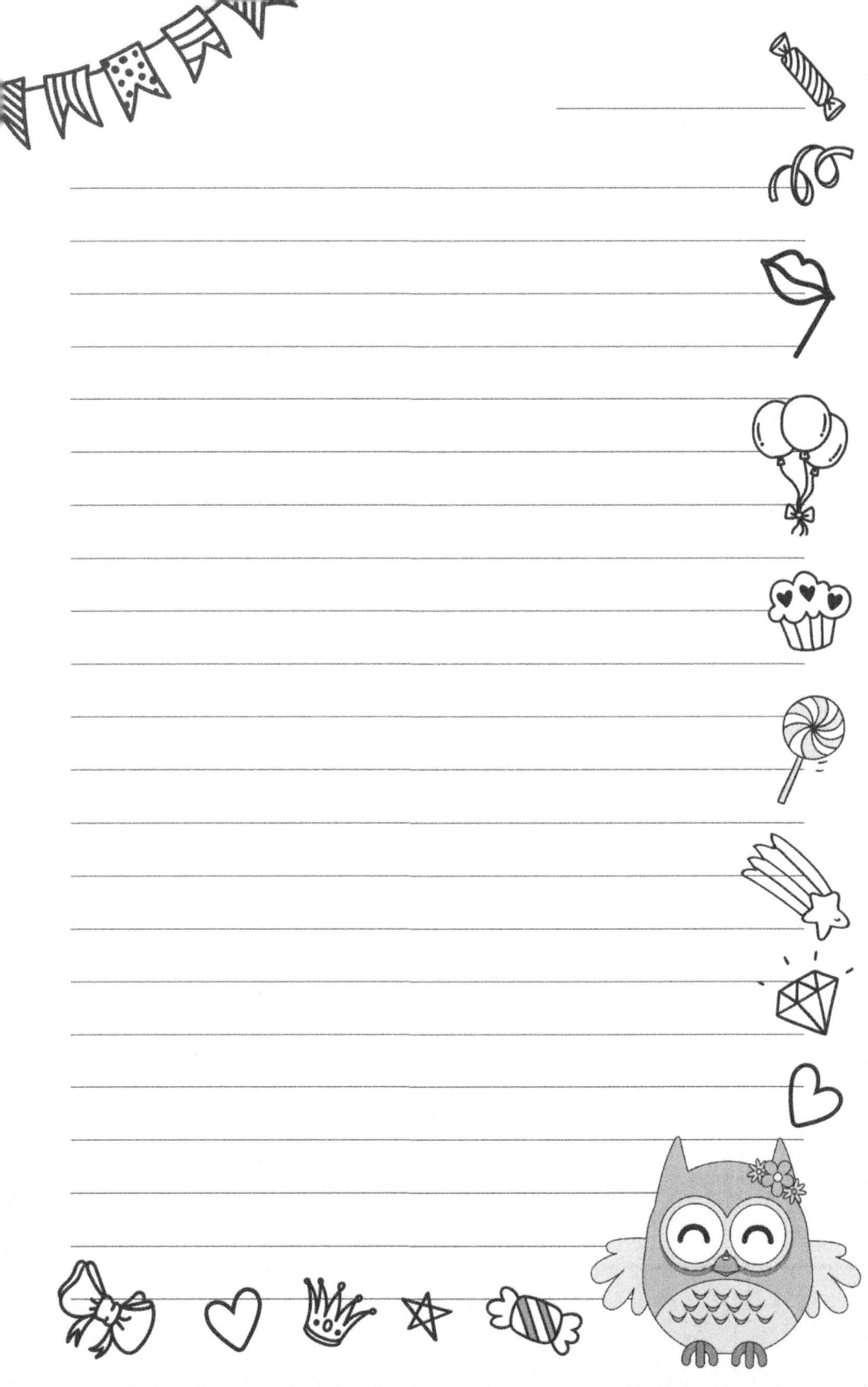

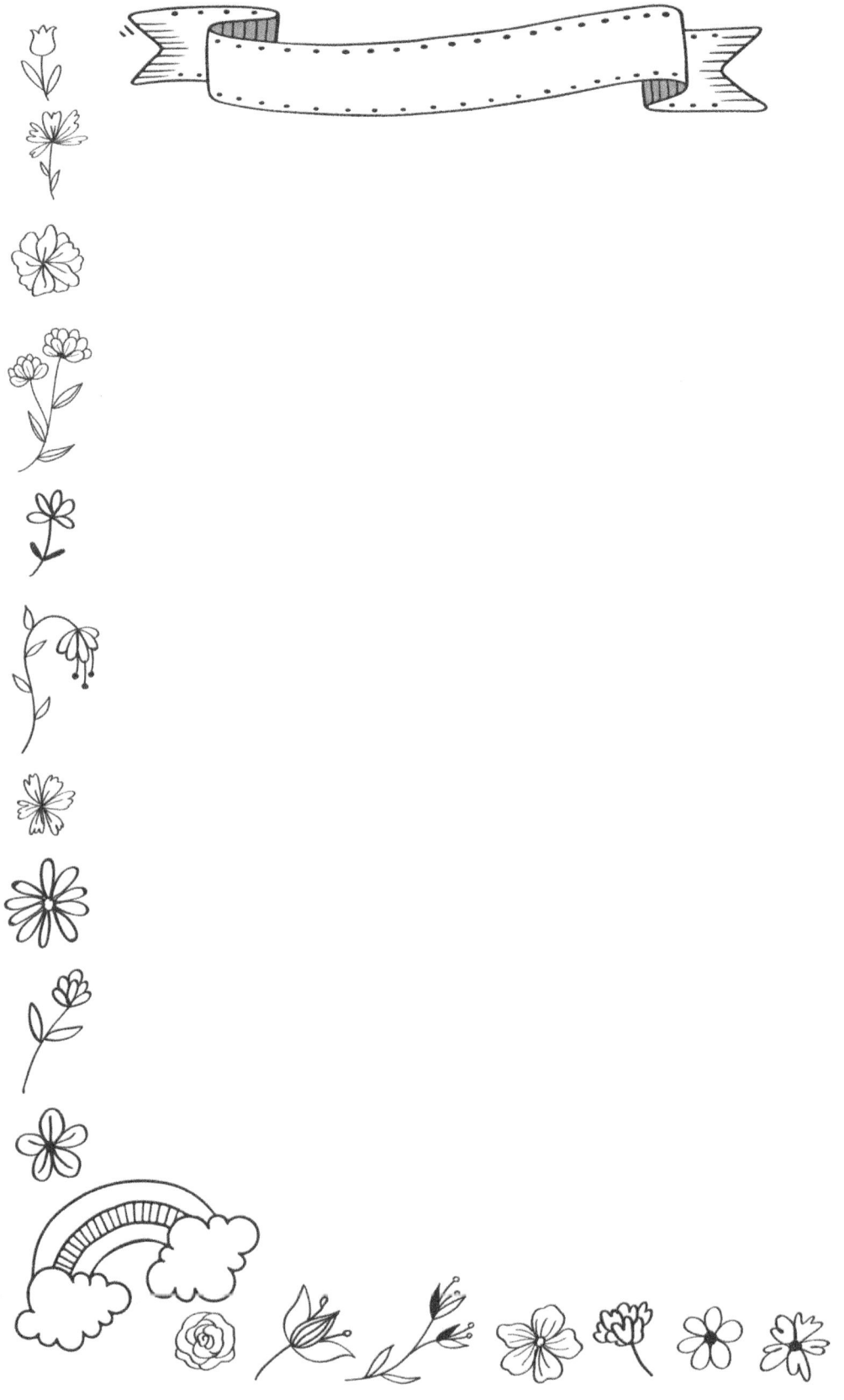

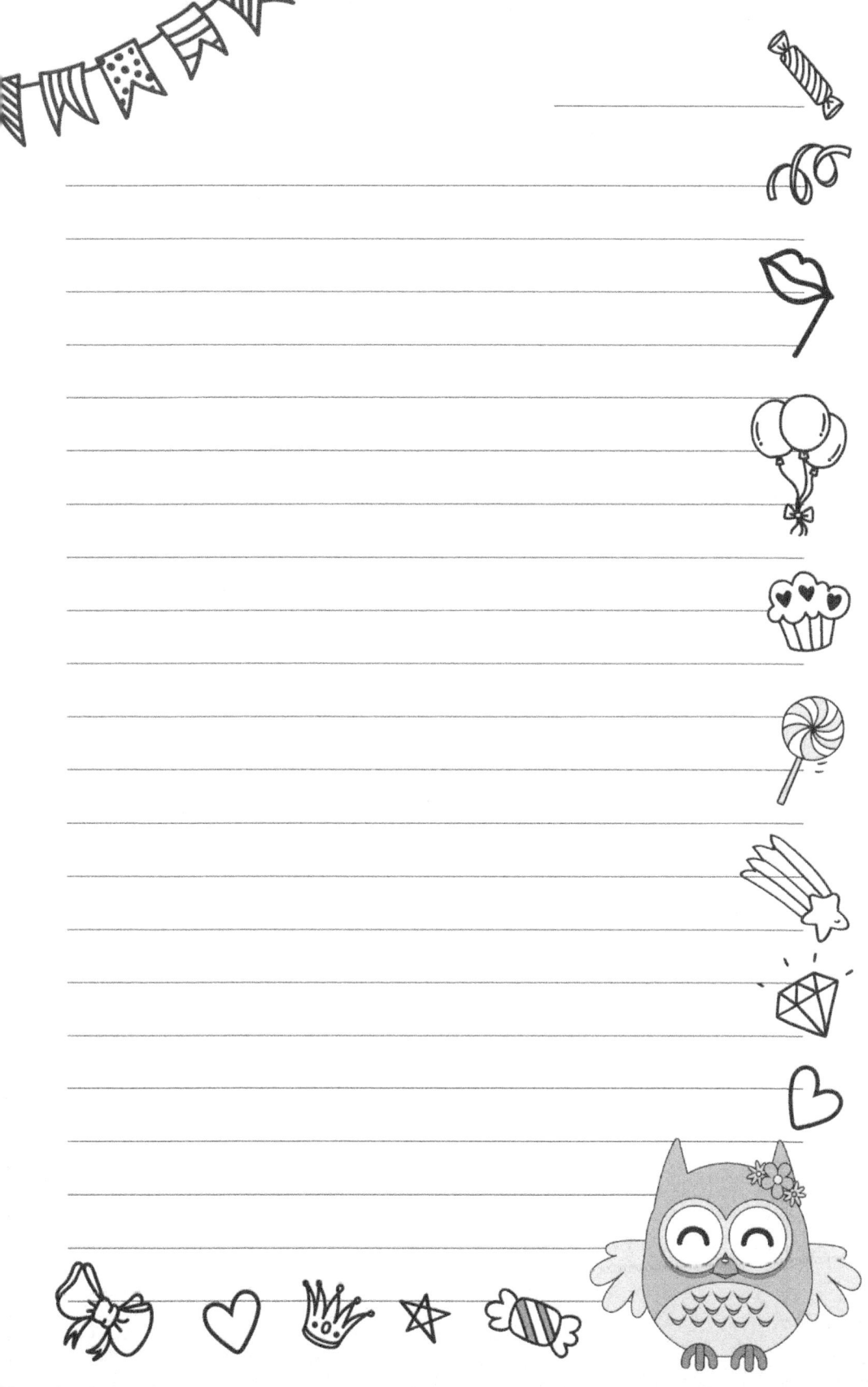

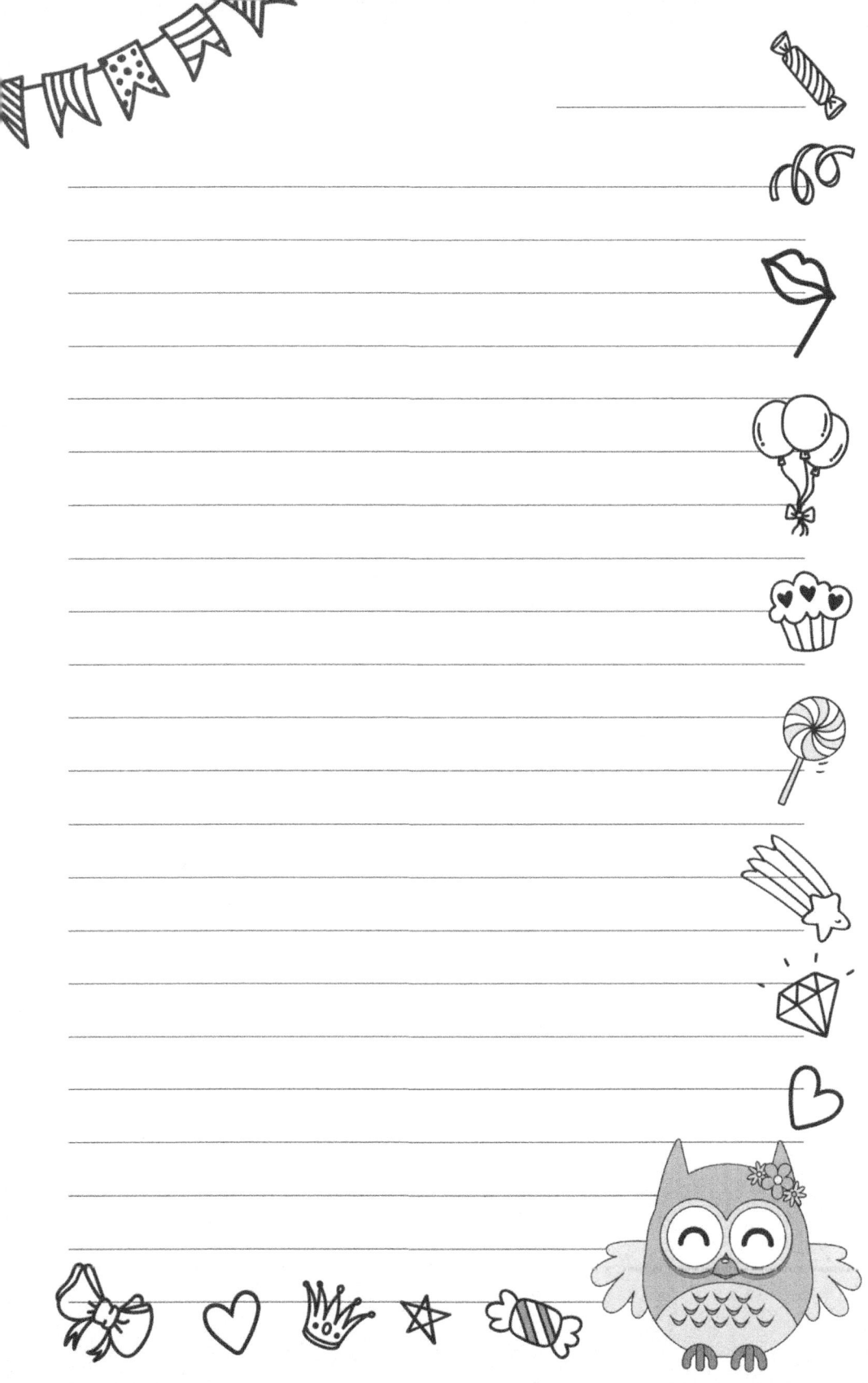

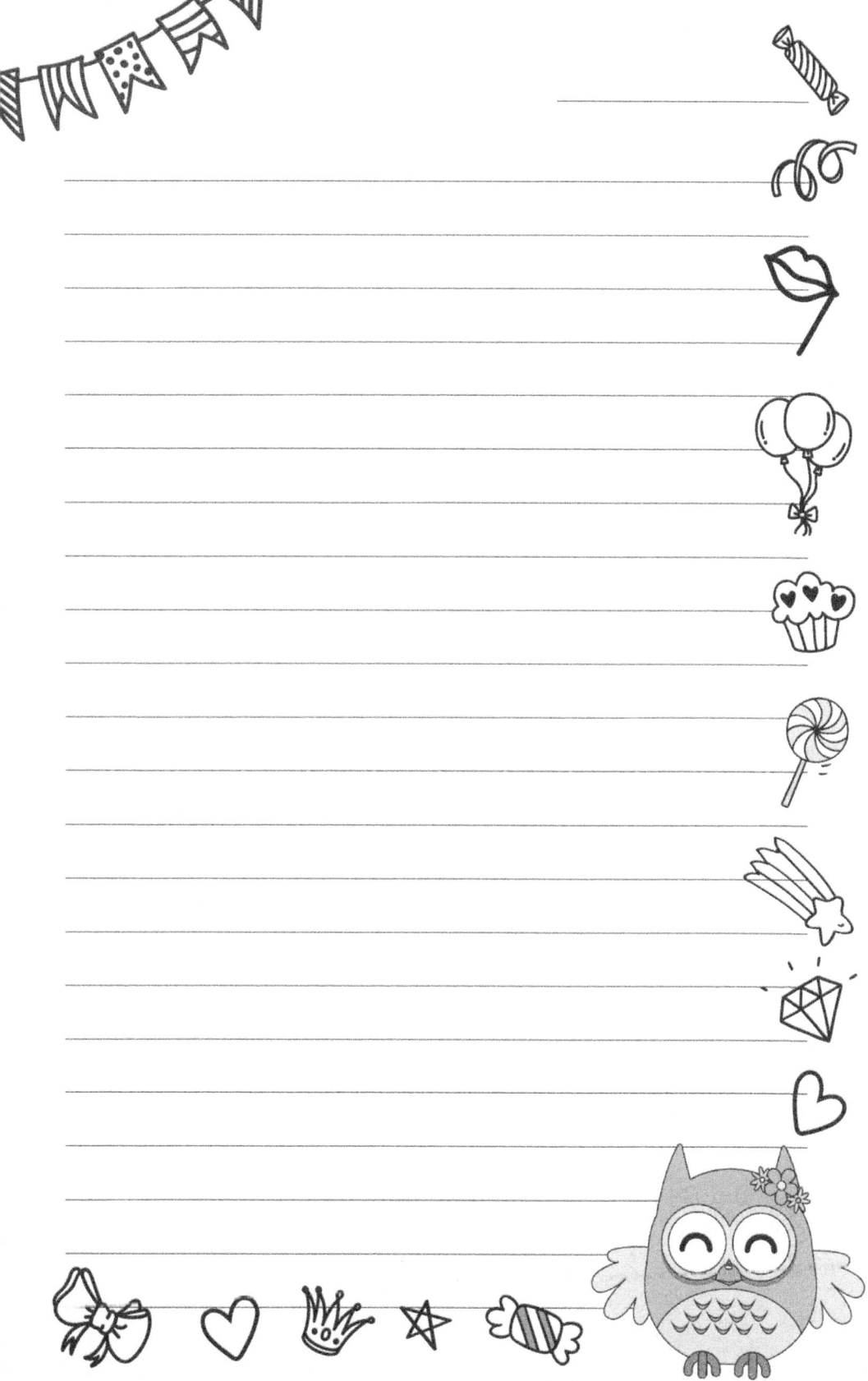

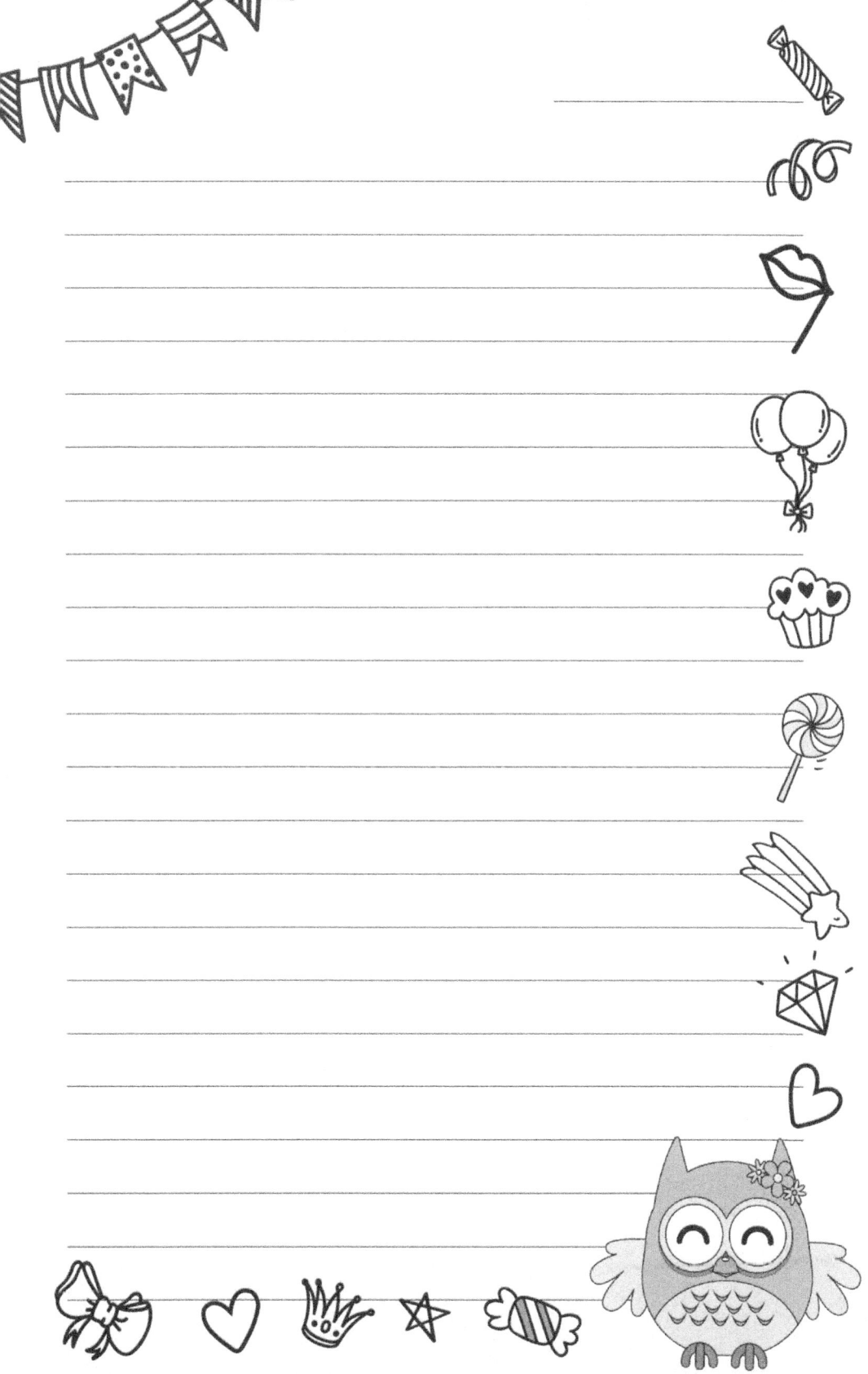

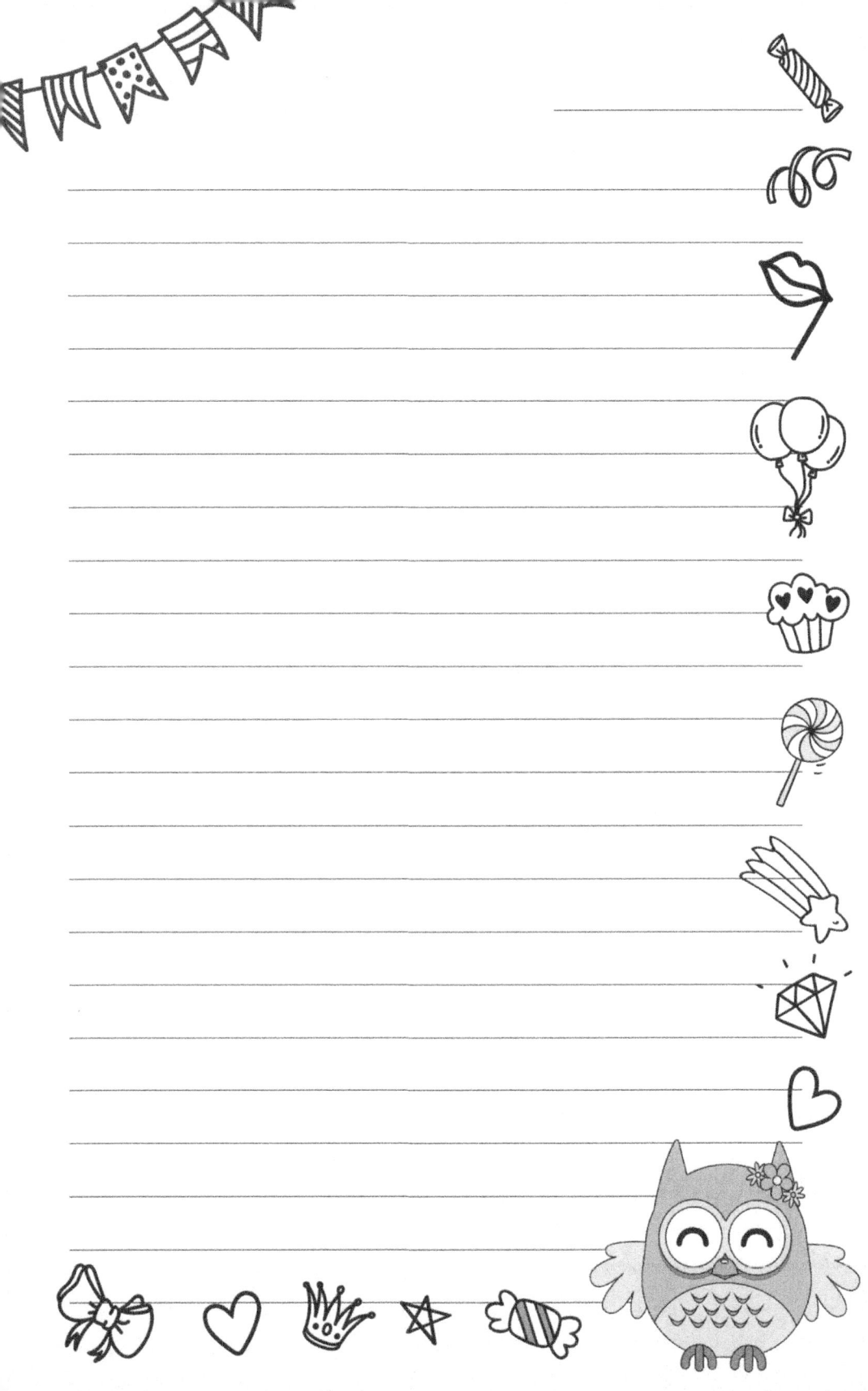

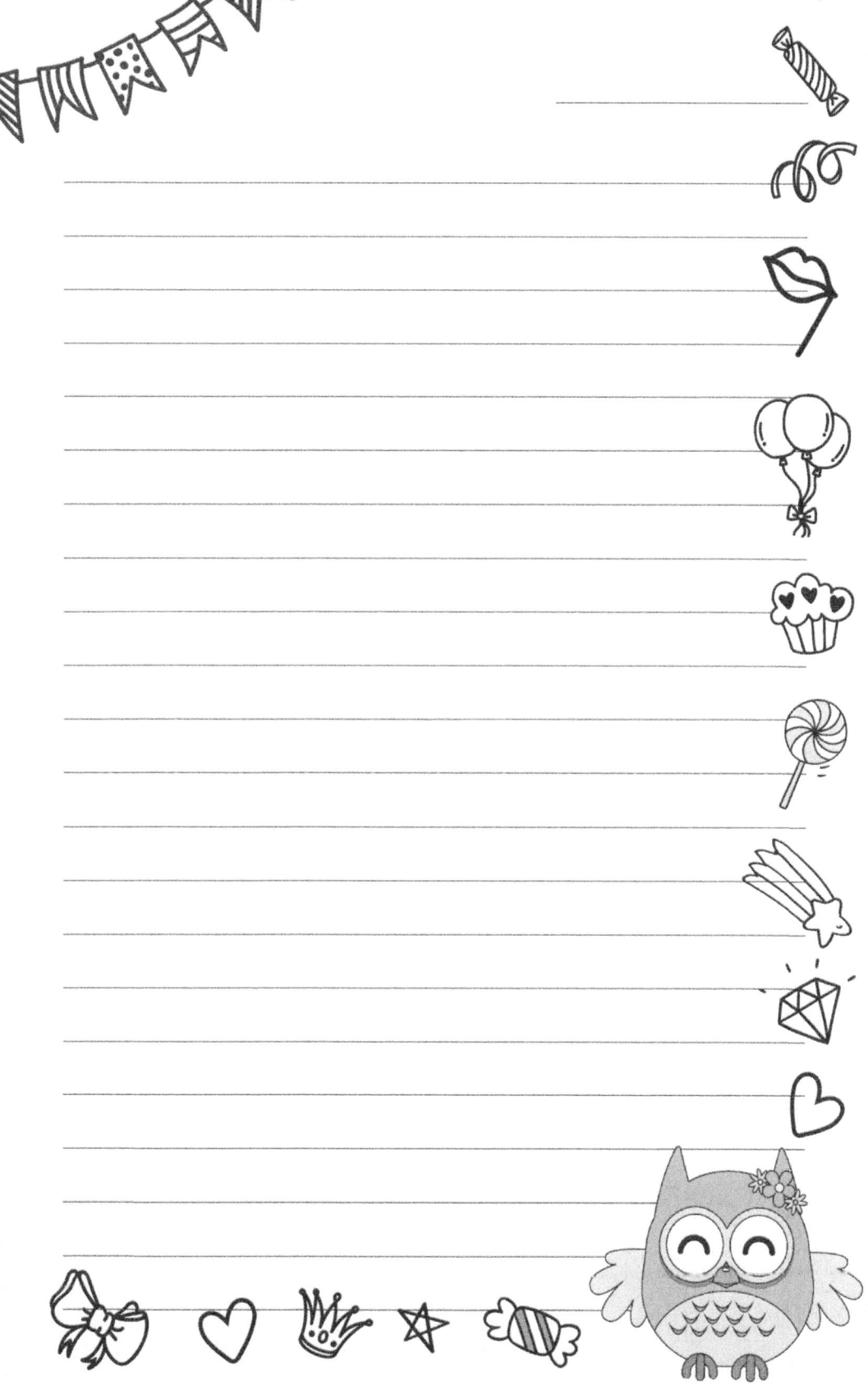

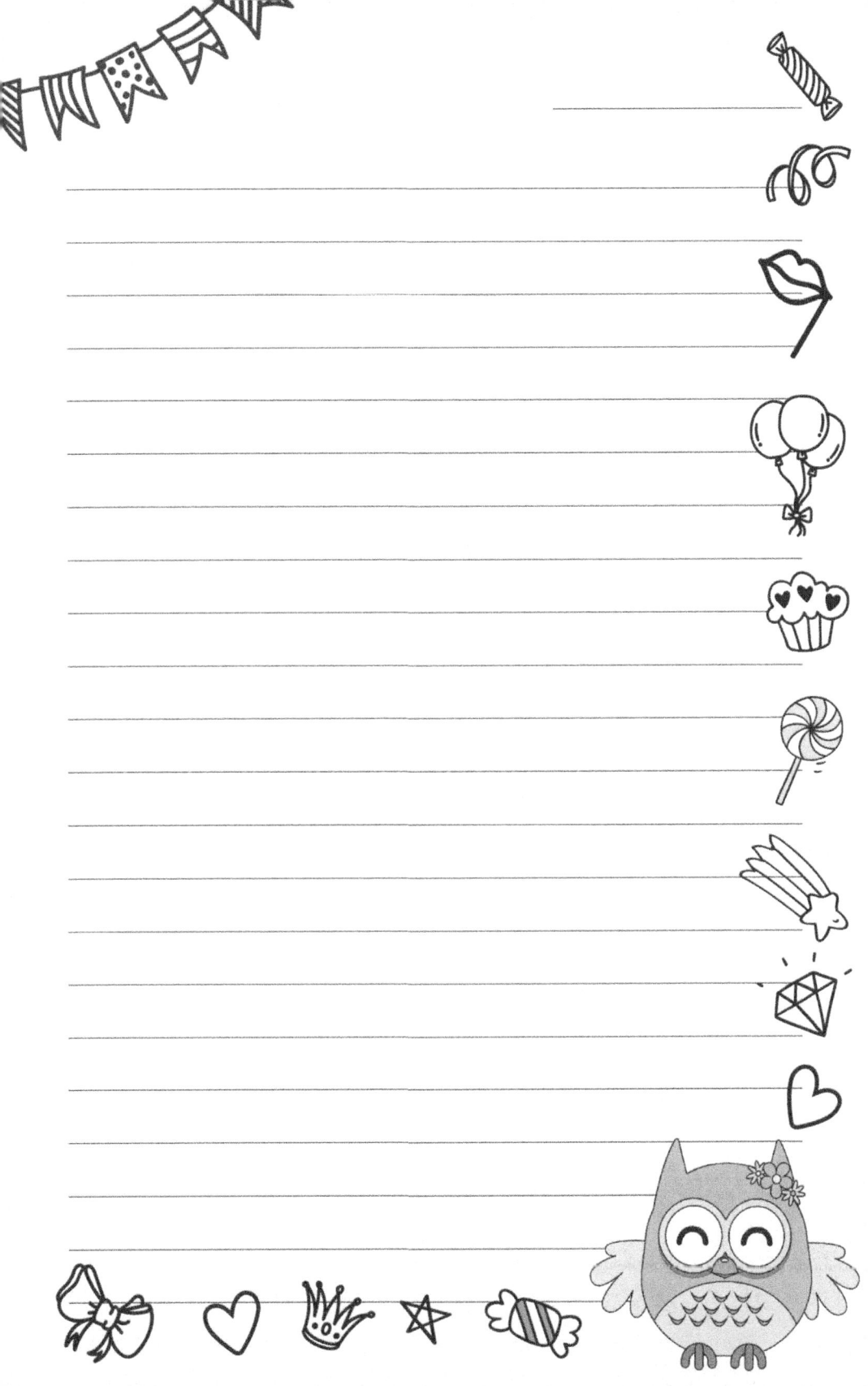

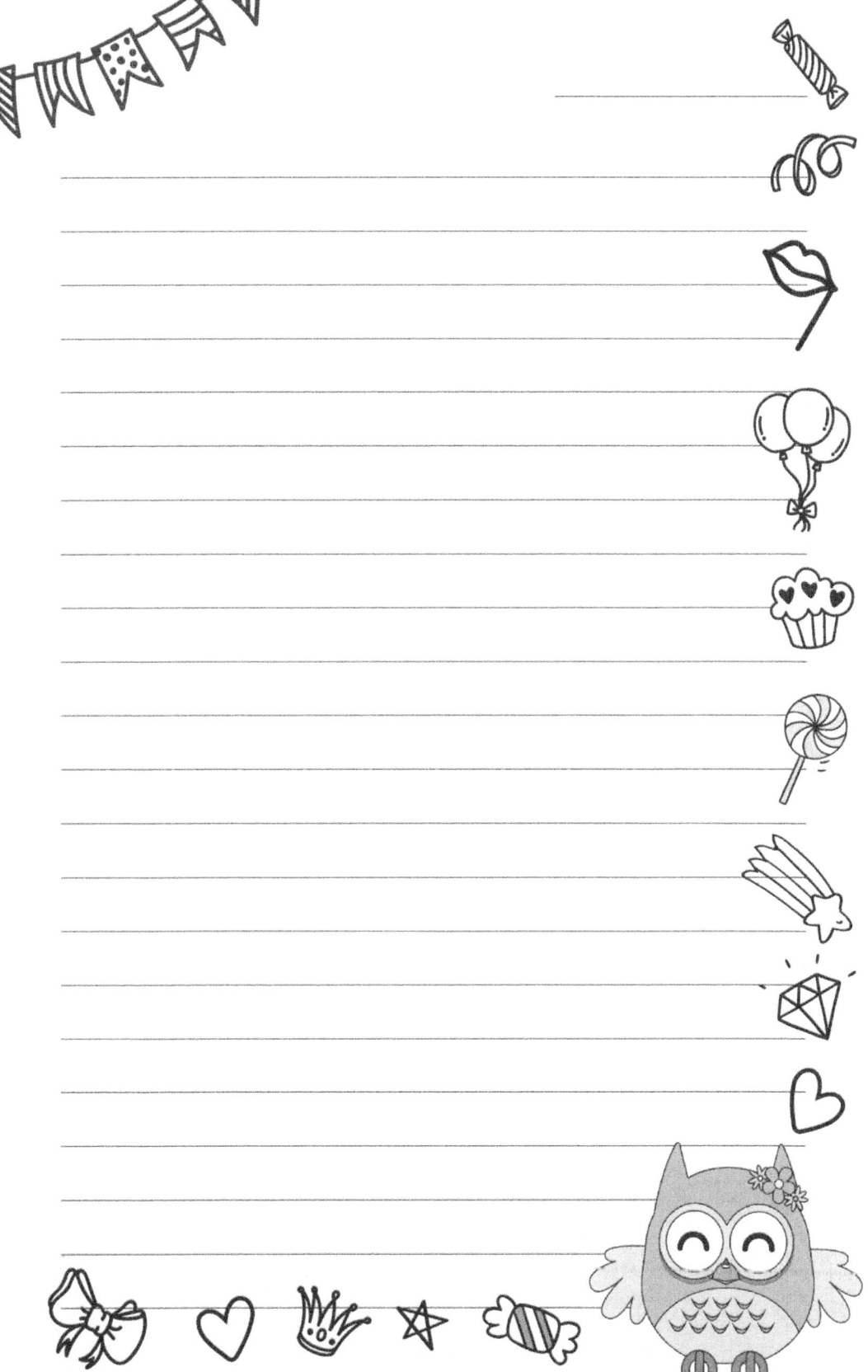

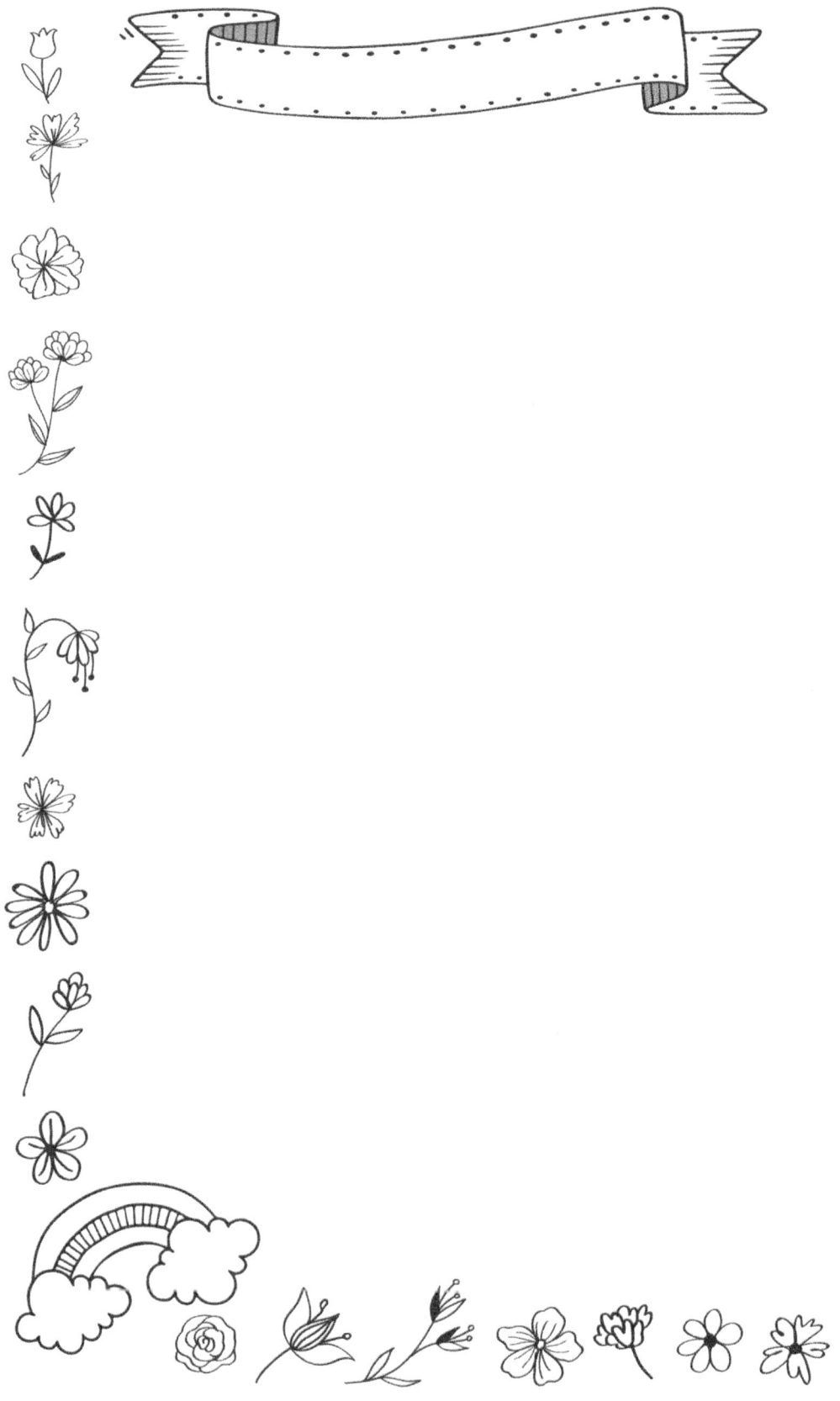

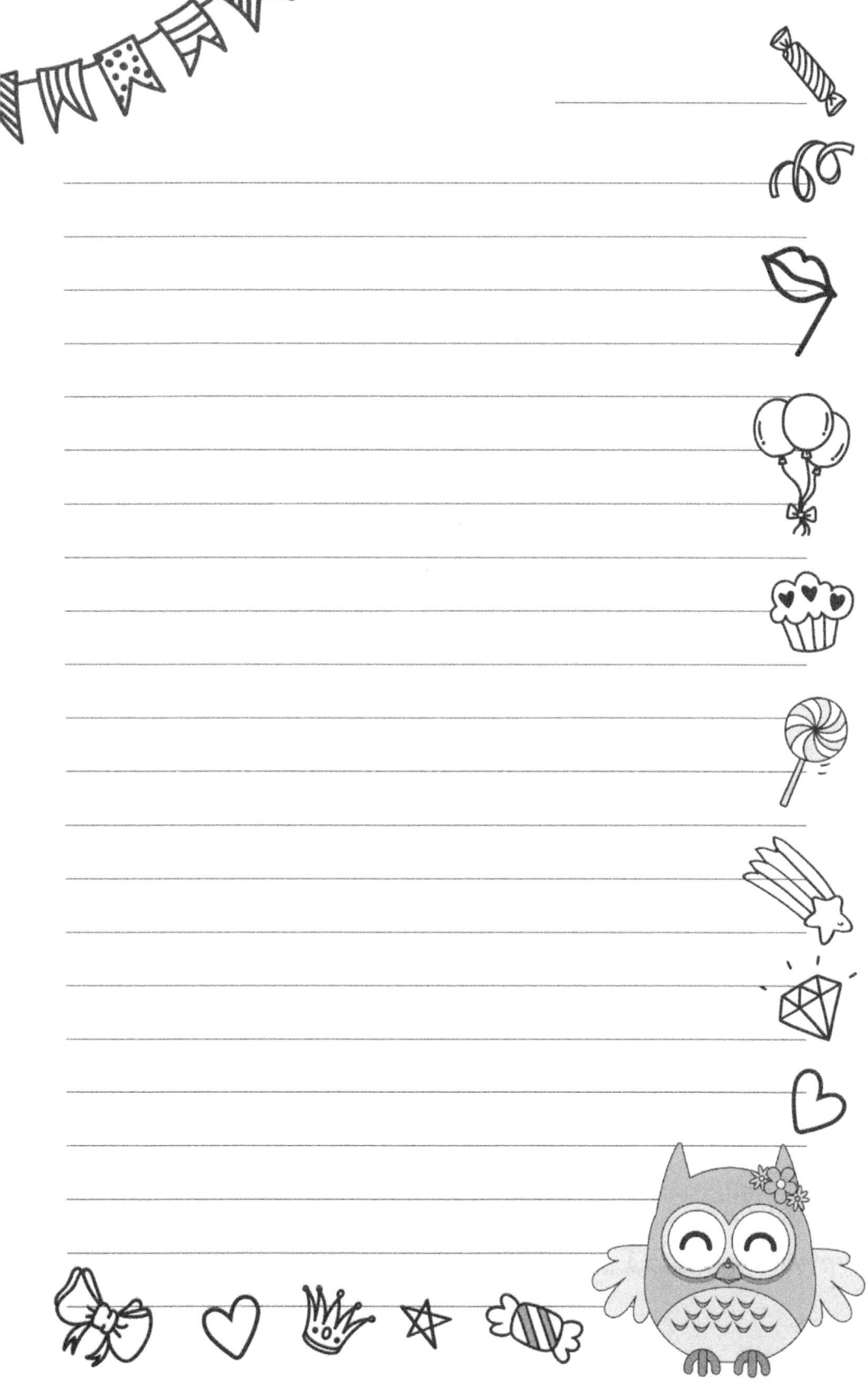

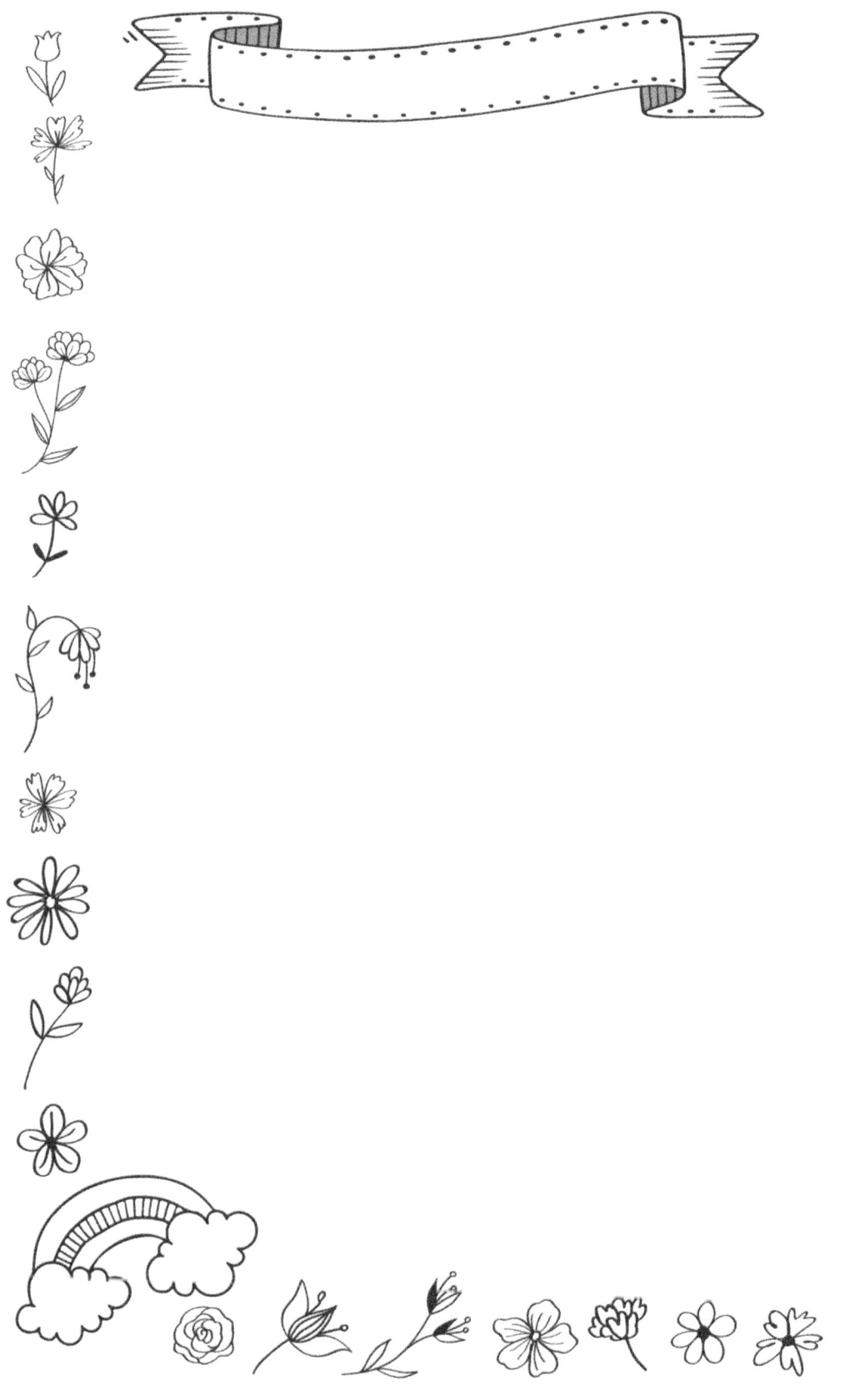

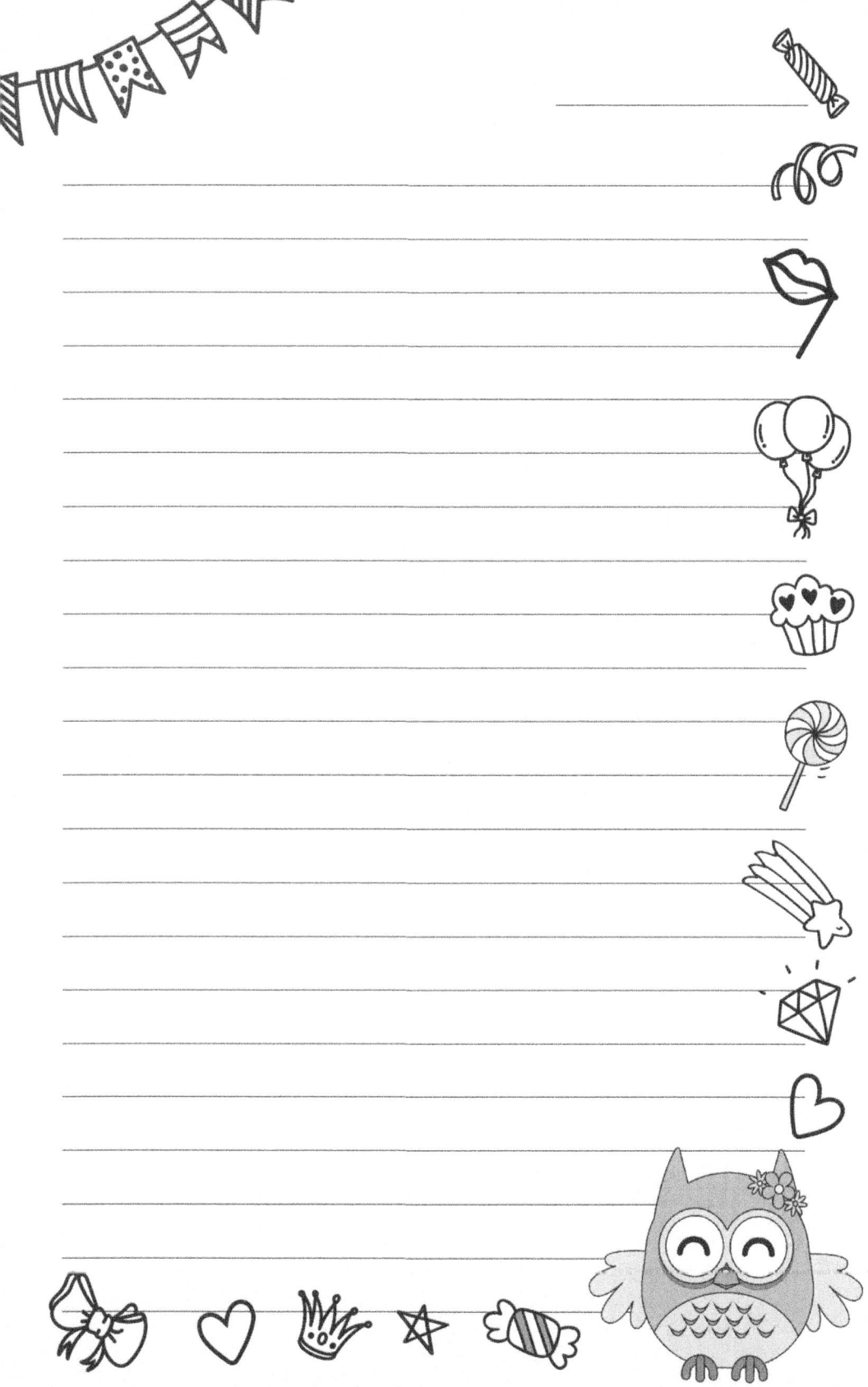

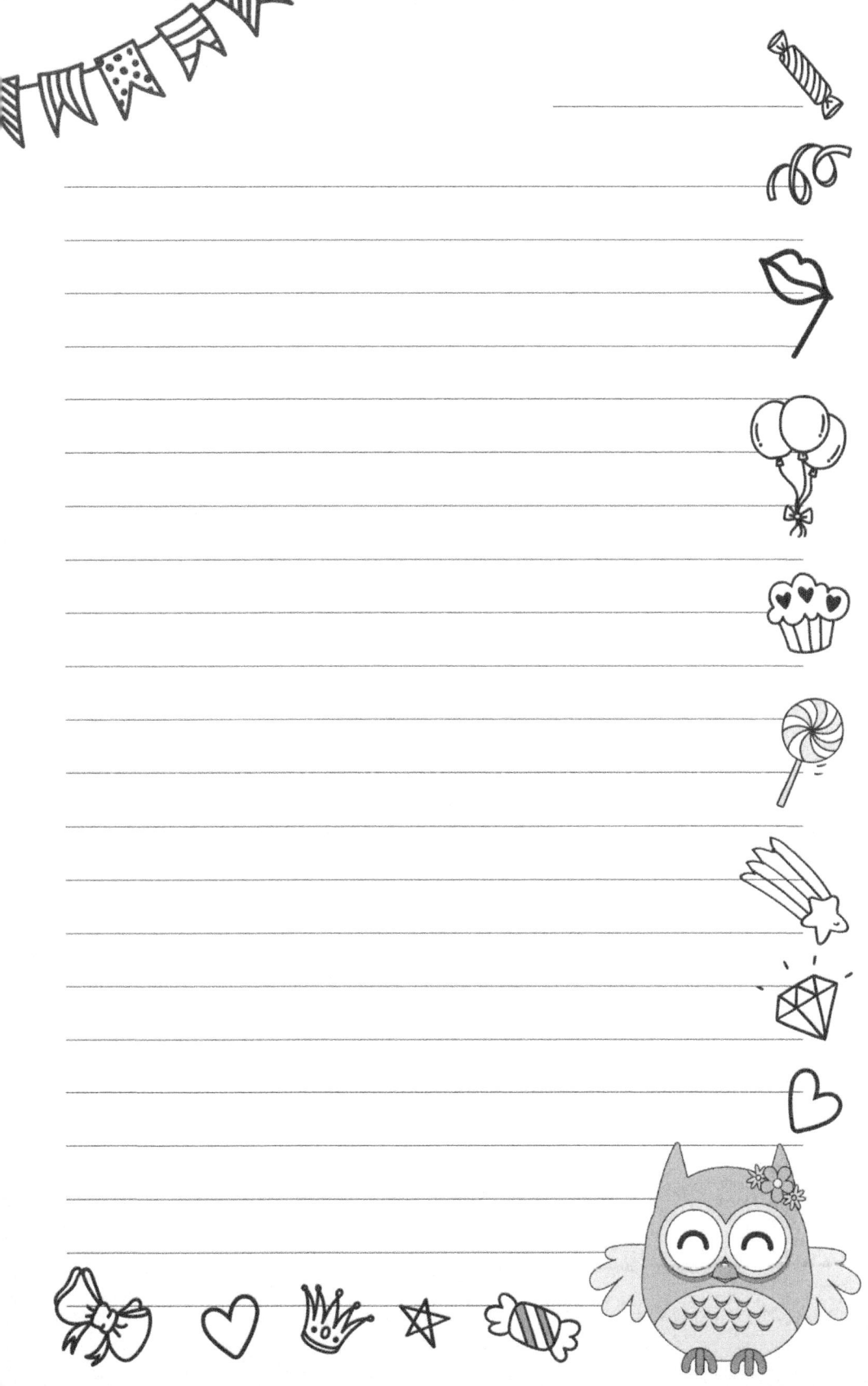

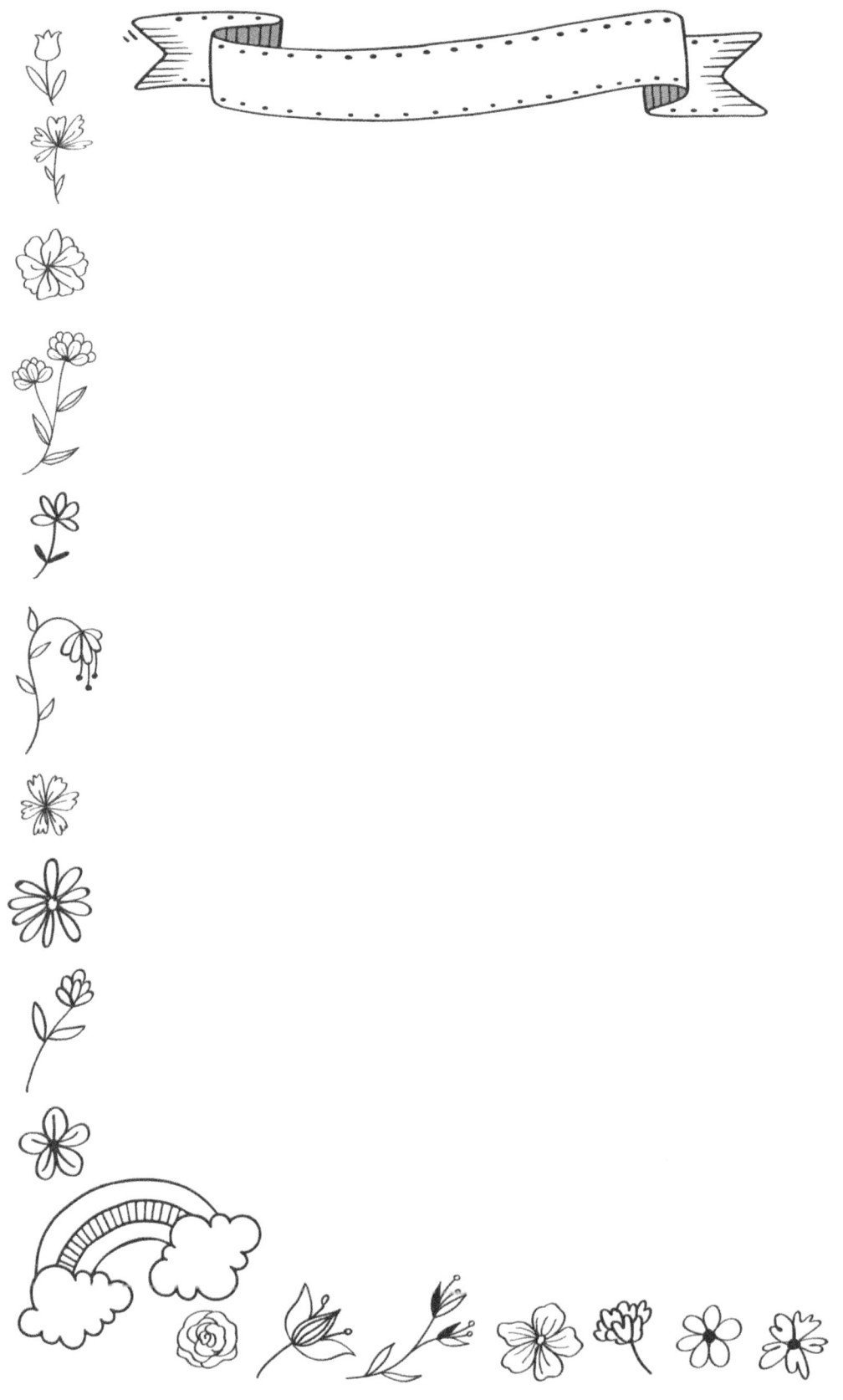

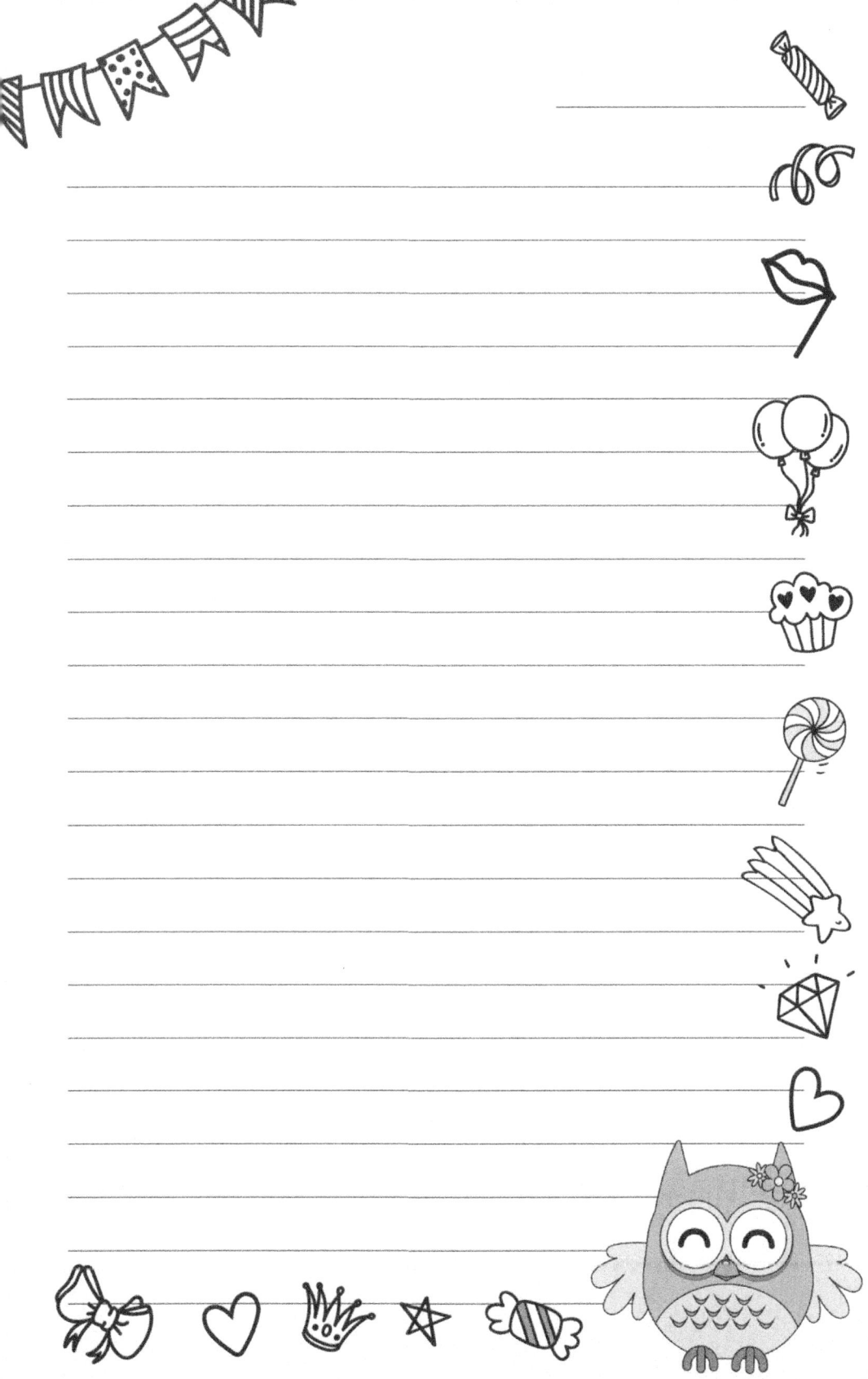

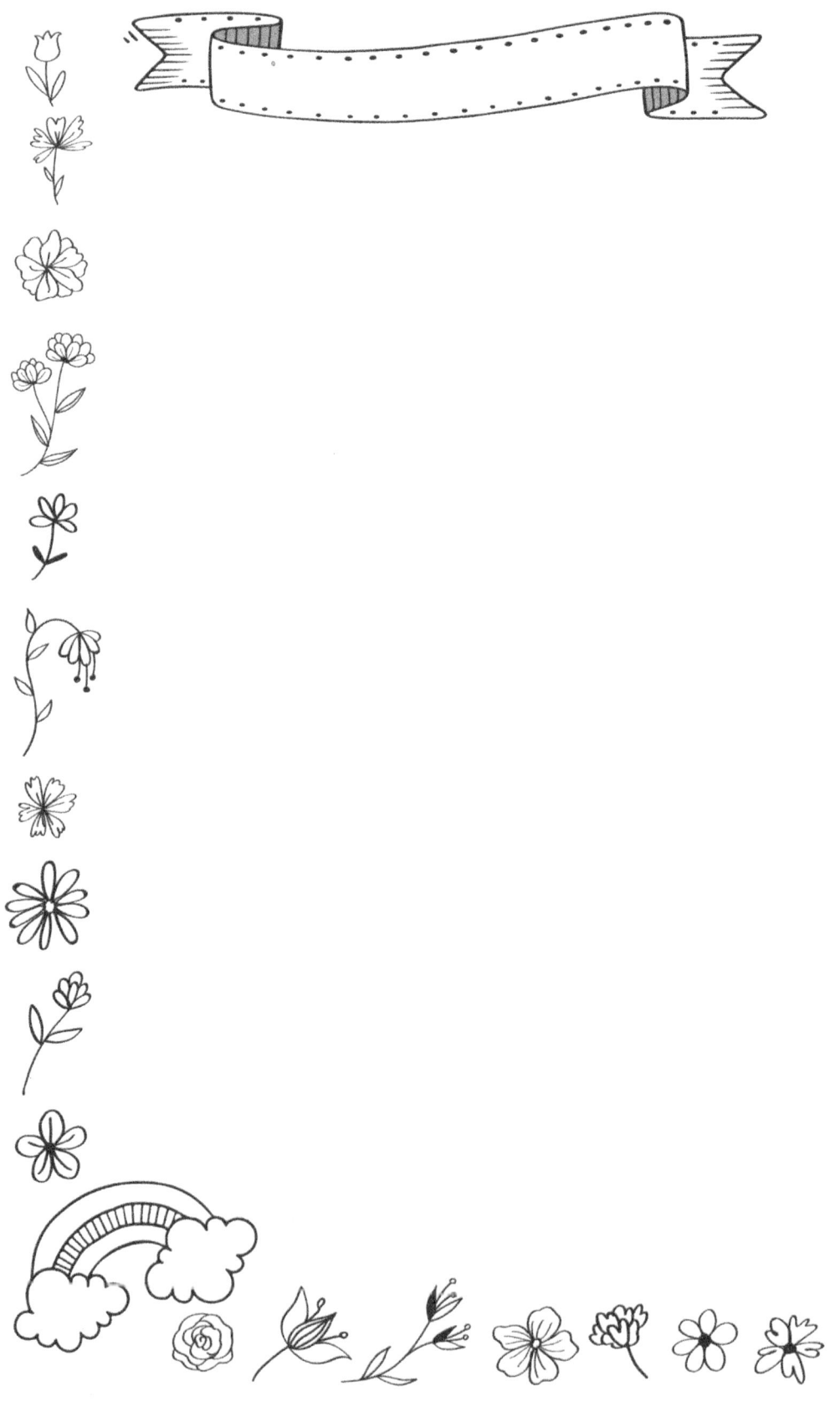

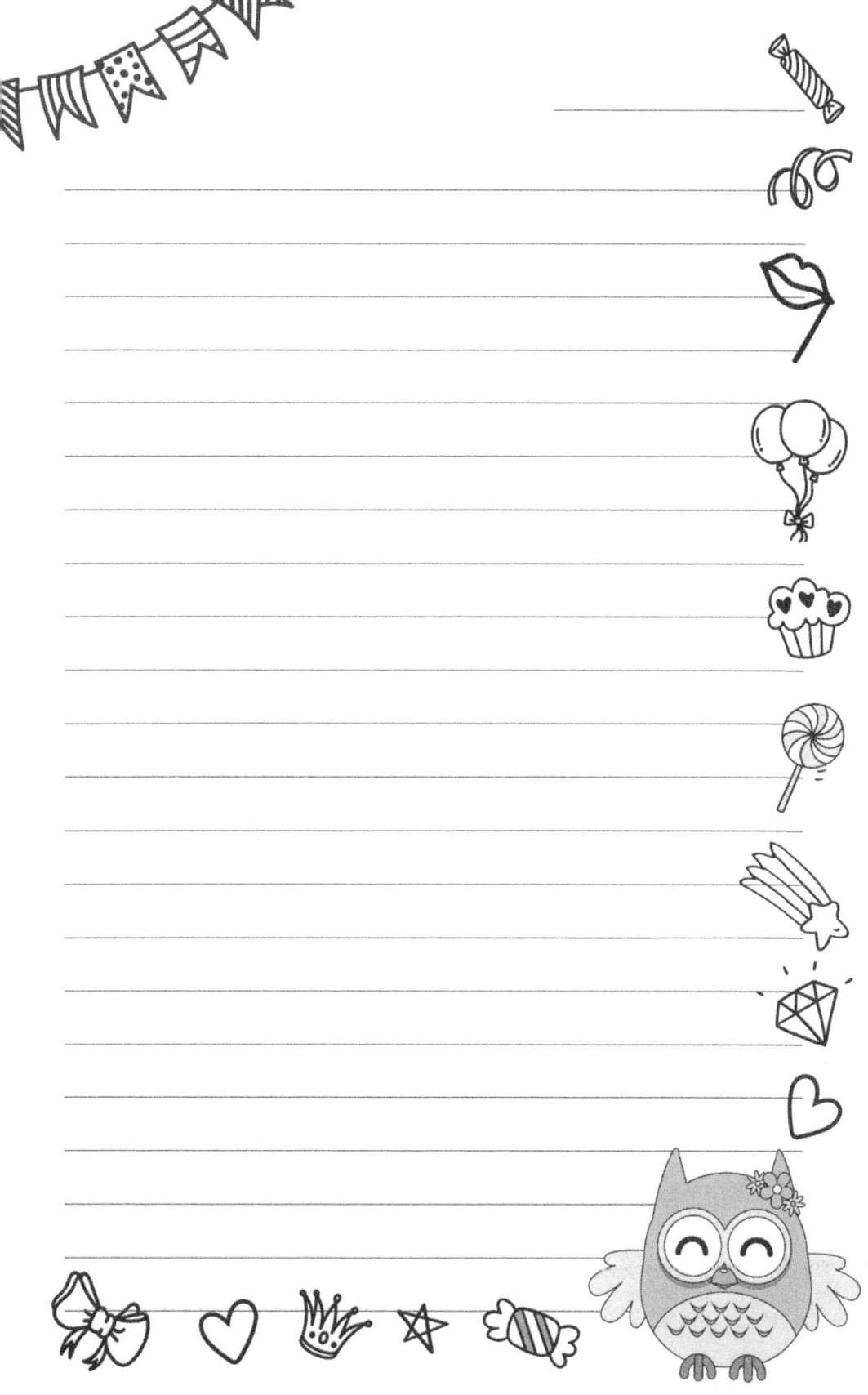

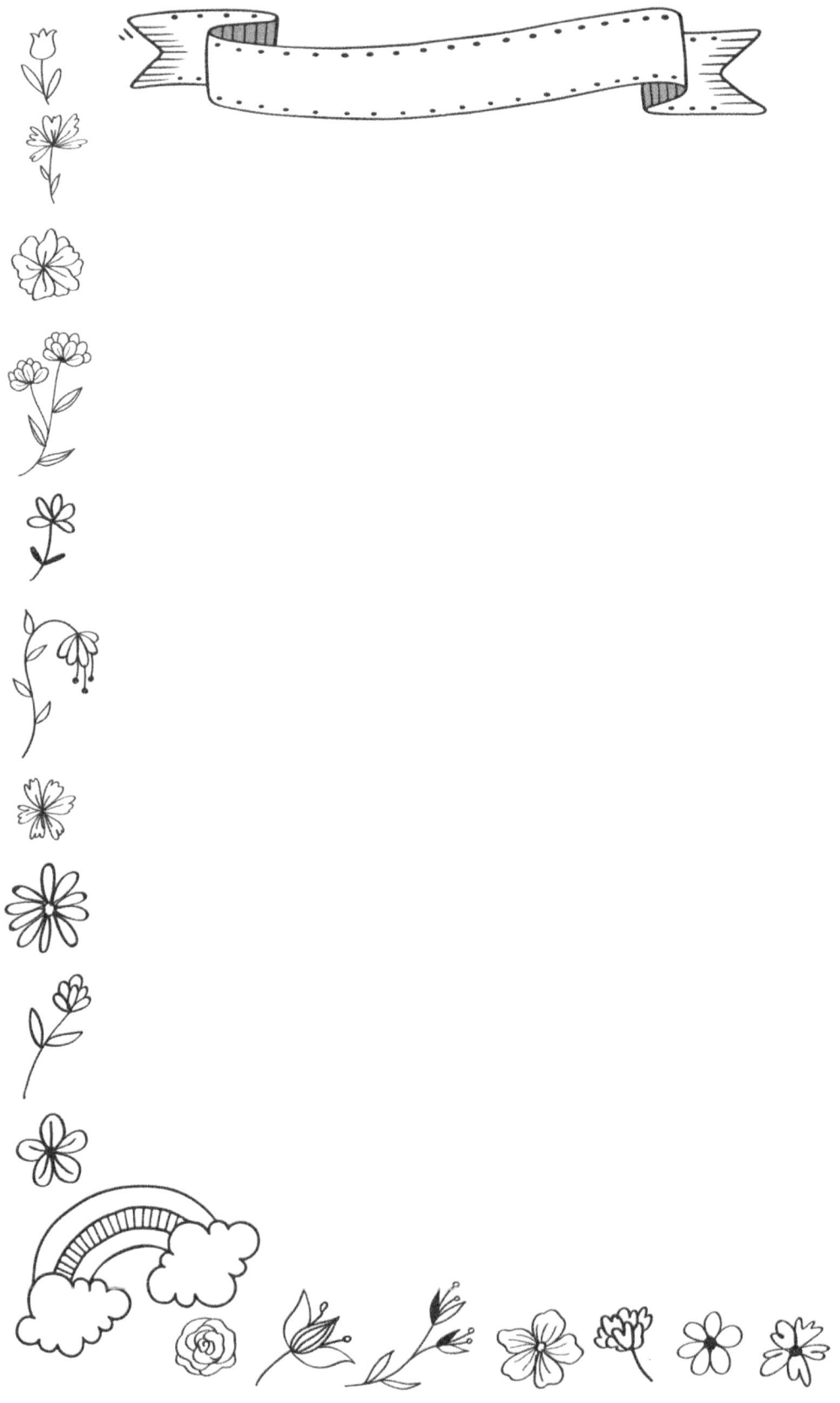

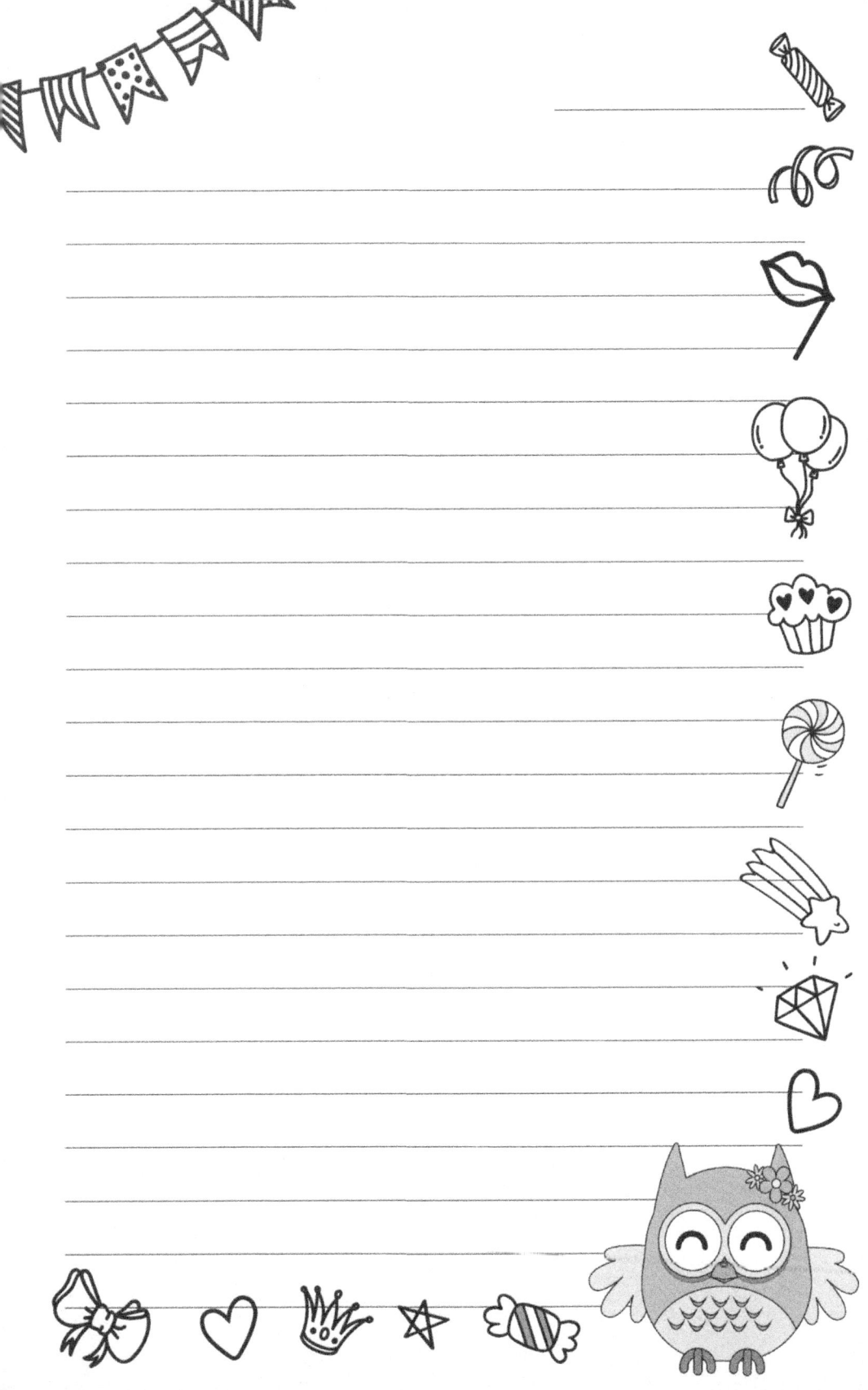

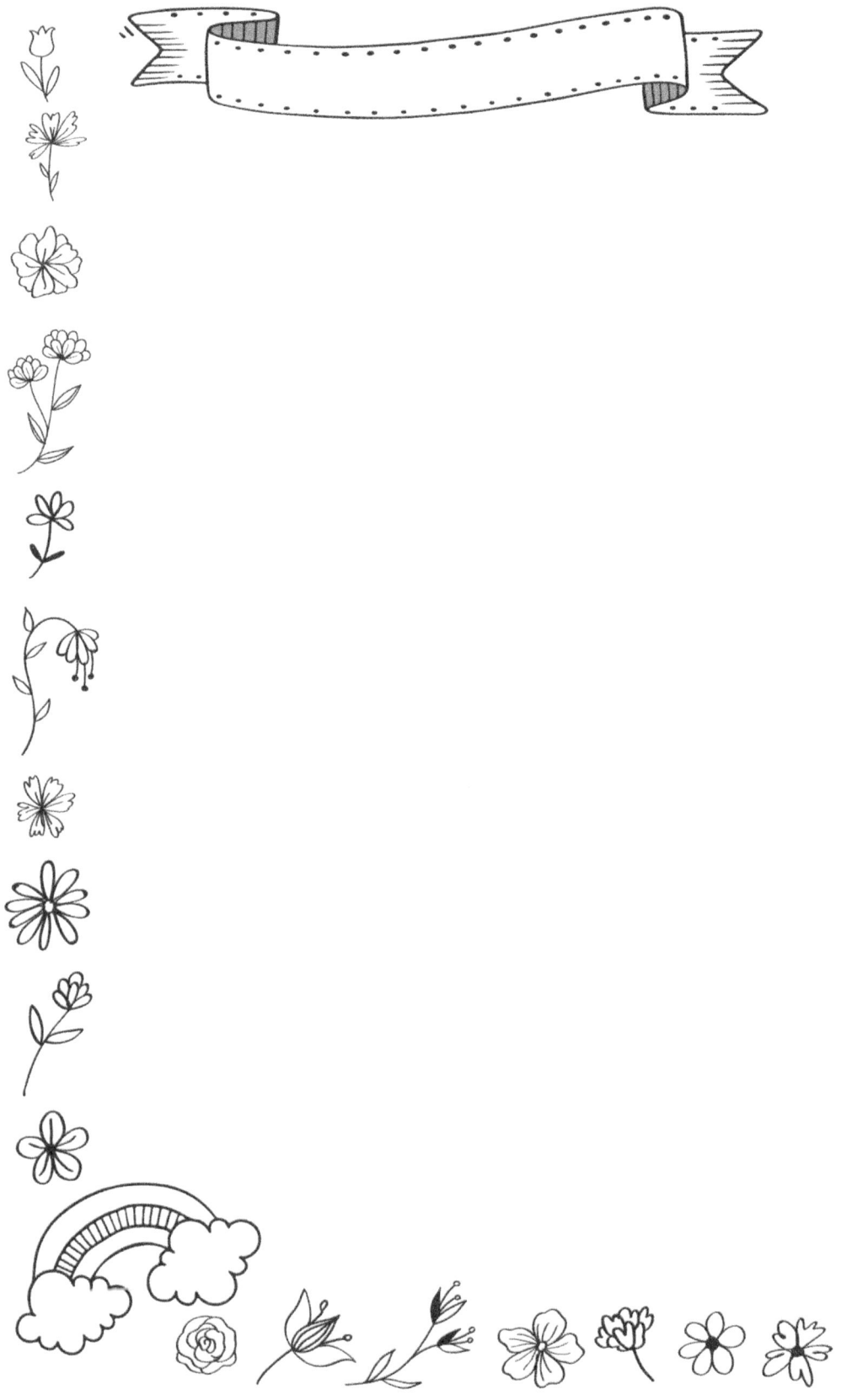

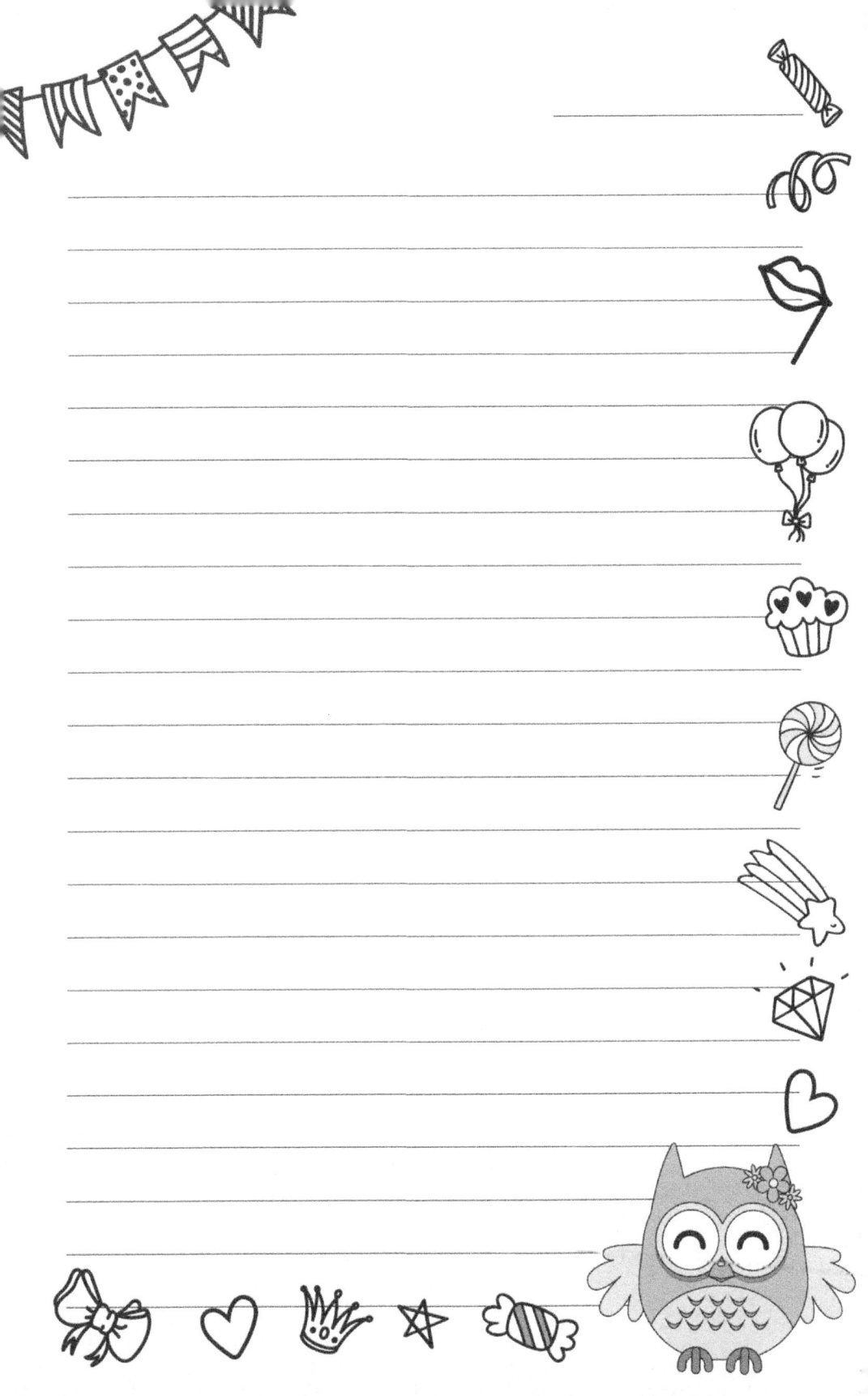

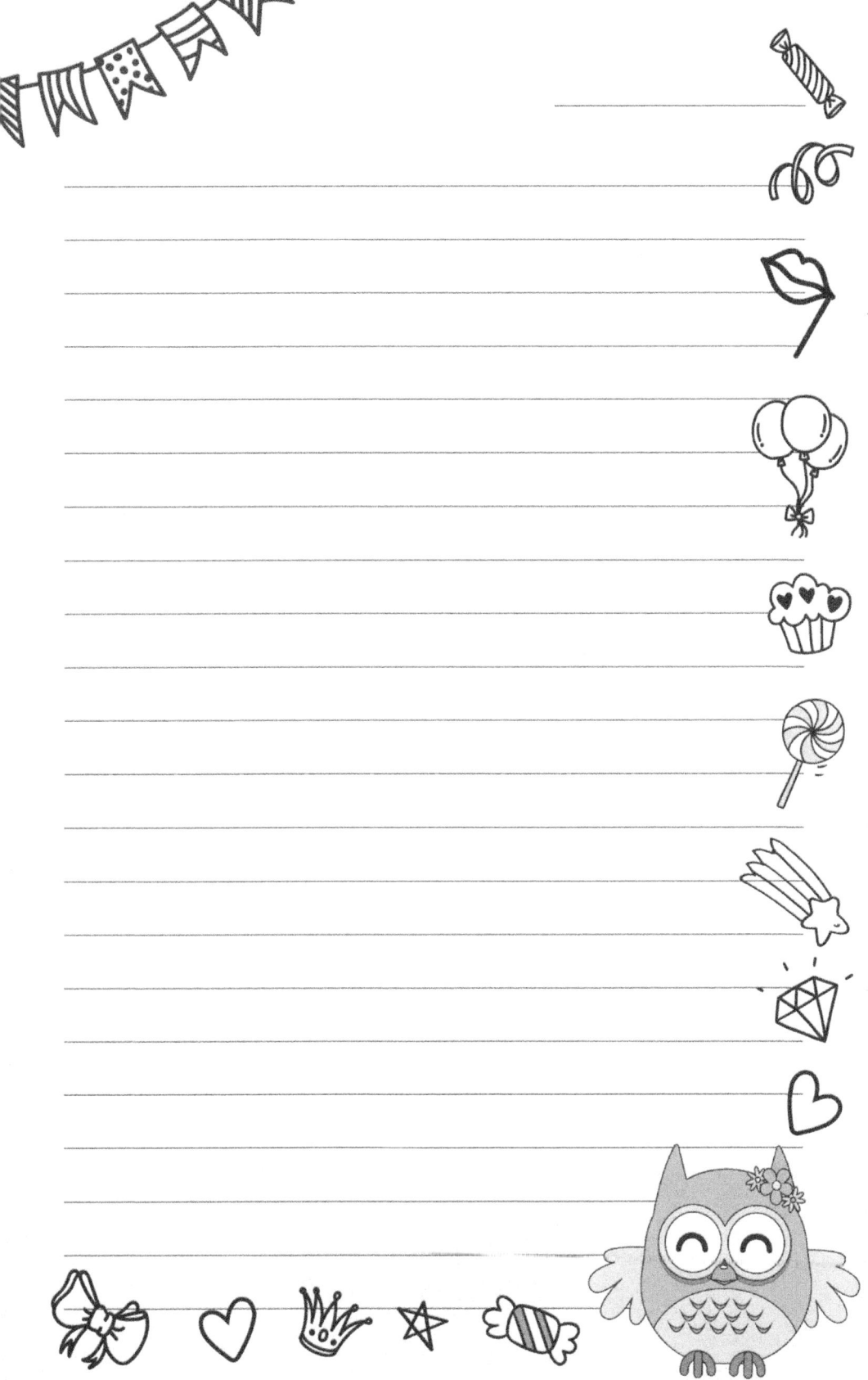

Made in the USA
Coppell, TX
05 June 2022